Corn Cuisine

60 Corn Dishes

A Bonanza for all Corn lovers

Prabhjot Mundhir

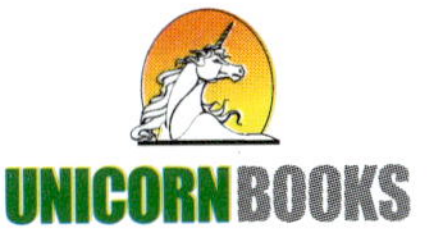
UNICORN BOOKS

Publishers
UNICORN BOOKS
J-3/16, Daryaganj, New Delhi-110002
☎ 23276539, 23272783, 23272784 • *Fax:* 011-23260518
E-mail: unicornbooks@vsnl.com
Website: www.unicornbooks.in • www.kidscorner.in

Distributors
Pustak Mahal, Delhi
Bangalore *e-mail*: pmblr@sancharnet.in • pustak@sancharnet.in
Mumbai *e-mail*: rapidex@bom5.vsnl.net.in
Patna *e-mail*: rapidexptn@rediffmail.com
Hyderabad *e-mail*: pustakmahalhyd@yahoo.co.in
London *e-mail*: pustakmahaluk@pustakmahal.com

ISBN 978-81-7806-144-3

Edition : February 2008

Printed at : Param Offsetters, Okhla, New Delhi-110020

Introduction

The History of Corn

"It was on November 5, 1492, that Columbus sent two of his sailors on an exploration trip into the interior of Cuba. They returned to report and brought back with them a grain which the natives called "maize" and it had a delicious taste. On Columbus' return to Europe, the cultivation and use of what was then called Indian corn spread rapidly over the then known world. Within one single generation it became a European food staple. And in two generations it spread into Tibet, India and Africa.

When European ships first arrived in China, they found that corn had preceded them and that already it was being taxed by the emperor."

"The Tehuacan valley caves of Mexico have furnished evidence for the continuous evolution of maize from 6000 BC to 4000 BC, from a pre-historic grass to a stage where the plants carried pods two centimeters long, which thereafter increased both in pod size and productivity. The ancestor is now believed to have been a perennial wild grain, teosinte (Zea mexicana) which hybridized with 'diploperennis', another perennial teosinte about 4000 years ago to trigger off an explosive evolution that led to 'zea mays', a cultivated plant. Each of the many forms of corn, sometimes stated to number seven, was associated with an ancient culture, like the Mayan, Aztec, Inca or Chibehan".

"However, there is some puzzling evidence regarding maize in India in pre-Columban time. Very primitive forms of maize have been found in hilly Sikkim, and carefully studied by many experts. They have been classified into 15 races; the question naturally arises as how too many forms with innumerable local names could have arisen in just 400 years from a single genetic source introduced from the New World.

A second finding is that of a pot-sherd dated 1435 from Kaundinyapur in Madhya Pradesh, which bears an impression on the clay strikingly akin to that of a maize cob with its orderly arrangement of grains. Again, pollen grains from a site in the Kashmir Valley of a very early date have been identified as those of maize.

Finally the temple of Somnathpur, just outside Mysore city, built in the 12th century AD, shows 92 female figures holding, in their right hand, an object that looks remarkably like a corncob. A European scientist has stated recently that he is quite positive that they represent heads of maize, some even being shown covered with a silky tassel at the apex.

On the other hand, it has been argued that the same object is found in a Rajasthan idol of about AD 800, and that it represents a Jain religious item or symbol of which we are unaware.

The term makkiyanah used in a grant of king Indrapala found in Guwahati has been identified with makhana, a prickly aquatic herb of the region whose seeds are roasted and eaten", writes Dr K. T. Achaya in his book *INDIAN FOOD – A Historical Companion*, while writing about the bounty from the New World.

"Corn or maize is also known as Indian corn and corn on the cob. This plant is of South American origin. It was cultivated by the Peruvians before the arrival of Spanish settlers.

Corn was introduced into France in the sixteenth century and many varieties are now grown there. It flourishes in the wine growing districts. Fresh corn on the cob is not much used in **French cooking.** In America, on the other hand, it is eaten in quantity", says *New Larousse Gastronomique,* the world's greatest cookery reference book, by Prosper Montagne.

Corn is relatively poor in nitrogenous substances, but quite rich in lipids and carbohydrates. Its flour makes bread which is very popular in America. It contains a high proportion of oil but does not keep. In some regions it is eaten as porridge or polenta, cakes and bread. The grains can be grilled, boiled or made into popcorn or cornflakes.

In Mexico where corn is the grain used for bread, they make delicious pancake bread called Tortillas (tor-tee-yahs), which accompany every meal. Historically, tortillas were made exclusively with cornmeal; this is the reason tortillas are an important part of the Mexican diet from a nutritional point of view. Unfortunately, these days in America or in Mexico, tortillas sold commercially are made of flour and not cornmeal. They are not only tasteless but their nutritional value is also zero.

Americans use the corn kernels for making soups, salads and steamed corn bread known as 'Corn Mush'. It is also known as Polenta, especially in **Italian cooking.** They also eat the corn-on-cob steamed and in the form of popcorns flavoured with various things. It is used to bake a variety of pies too. And of course, the cornflakes can't be forgotten.

Chinese use the corn mainly for making soups along with meats and vegetables.

In India corn is used in various forms. Since time immemorial, in North India it is eaten either in the form of **Popcorns** or roasted **Corn on the cob (Bhutta)** or in the form of the famous **Makki-ki-Roti** made of cornmeal.

In Western and Southern India it is mainly eaten roasted or boiled **Corn on the cob** and cornmeal mixed with fenugreek leaves as **Bhakri,** grated corn mixed with potatoes, etc., and deep fried as **Corn patties** for snacks and boiled corn on cob pieces placed in coconut gravy as **Bhutta Salan.**

In the Eastern part of the country, corn kernels are used mainly in **Soups** and stir-fried dishes like **Makai Ghoogni.** People over there too enjoy steamed and roasted **Corn on the cob.**

Corn oil is used to cook food and **Corn flour** to make Custard powders and to thicken soups, gravies or puddings all over the country as it is done in the rest of the world. Of course, a variety of **Cornflakes** are eaten with milk or milk and fruits for breakfast in India as all over the world.

In India, a hard variety of Cornflakes is deep-fried and mixed with other Farsan items to make **Chewda** (a famous Indian dry snack which has a long shelf life and is exported to many countries). Well-seasoned corn stuffing is used to fill **Samosas, Spring rolls** and so many other snacks that are fried. A number of other dishes are also prepared with it. In the last twenty years or so, **Baby Corn** has become very popular and is used now in various forms. Commercially, too, it is being used for snacks and mixed vegetables, etc. Hence, almost after 600 years of its advent, **Corn has really become 'a grain of today'** and is eaten globally in one or the other form.

Important Information

"Freshly ground cornmeal, either white or yellow, has 41.7% Protein in every edible pound of corn. It is rich in Calcium, Phosphorus, Potassium, Vitamin A and natural unsaturated oil", says Dr. Paul C. Bragg, America's health pioneer. Corn/Maize also contains Vitamin B and one of the sources is whole grains or whole grain cereals. Of the other minerals, whole maize contains Chlorine, Magnesium, Molybdenum, Silicon, Sodium, Sulphur, Vanadium, Zinc and Amino Acids.

In short, corn is considered good for the heart, skin and glowing hair. It is good for heart muscles, stimulates brain action, aids digestion especially of carbohydrates, reduces fatigue, increases stamina, prevents constipation, and prevents premature ageing by increasing mental alertness. It has a mild diuretic effect. It helps to maintain the normal red blood count and improves circulation, and promotes a healthy skin. It also prevents oedema or fluid retention in connection with heart ailments.

Acknowledgement

I would like to dedicate this book to my father late Mr. Prithvi Singh Kalsi. This book is for all the **Corn lovers** living in India and abroad, who love it and know its importance in daily diet. I must thank all those users of my previous books, my family and my well wishers who inspired me to develop the present book for them.

Above all, I can't forget to thank my husband Wg.Cdr Mandhir Singh for his unrelenting support at each stage of developing this book and be the best critic too.

I am grateful to my publishers who have faith in me.

—*Prabhjot Mundhir*

Preface

After the 600 hundred years of its advent, 'corn' became 'a grain of the day' and is eaten in many forms globally. In the introduction of the book it is already explained how it was eaten in most of the countries in the past; but now with the popularisation of 'Mexican food' and introduction of many multinational companies and their products, it is becoming more popular with the youth of the world. Presently, the mushrooming of the 'Corn Clubs' all over the big cities is also responsible to make it more popular. I came across many young people who do not like the products made of cornmeal

traditionally but love the tasty preparations of corn kernels sold commercially by these clubs. No doubt, Popcorns are loved by young and old alike everywhere.

Earlier in India, urban society used to believe that corn is the staple of the rural folks, as a result very few people used to relish many of the dishes prepared from cornmeal, whereas most of them always enjoyed popcorns and roasted or boiled corn on the cob. Now as the awareness grows about corn's benefits, I am sure this 'grain of the day' will be the choice of more and more number of children and young people.

Here, in this book, the traditional recipes of corn are included and some recipes are developed on the basis of its use internationally. As a result, you will come across the recipes developed from corn kernels, cornmeal, corn dalia, cornflakes and baby corn to suit the universal taste. Each recipe included in the book is tried and tested; easy to cook and provides wonderful variety and nourishment to your meals. Of course, some commercially available items are not included purposely.

Happy time corn lovers. Just follow the recipes carefully and I am sure not only you can satisfy your own taste buds but also satiate the desire of your loved ones for variety in food containing corn. My own grandchildren, aged two and three love eating baby corn and corn kernels in any form. Since I call the corn a grain of the day, I presume it is for the present generation and posterity.

Note: In this book, for many dishes corn is steamed in the microwave, or dishes are partly cooked in the microwave only to save time in the kitchen, otherwise corn can be steamed on the gas stove in the traditional way; and the whole procedure can be followed correctly and entire cooking can be done without a microwave. You can bake the dishes in an electric oven and that may take a little more time.

Each dish featured in this book serves 4 to 6 persons.

Contents

Soups 15

Salads 27

Snacks 41

Snacks 57

Main Course 73

Side Dishes

Main Course 87

Roties and Pulao

Main Course 99

Baked Dishes

Main Course 115

Non-vegetarian

Sweet Treats 131

Dressings for Salads 143

References 148

Soups

- Tomato and Corn Chowder
- Corn Dumplings Soup
- Chinese Chicken Corn Soup
- Chicken, Shrimps and Sweet Corn Soup
- Corn and Mushroom Chowder

1. Tomato and Corn Chowder

- Tomatoes ... *2 large*
- Tinned Corn cream-style ... *1 cup*
- Corn kernels ... *½ cup*
- Cornmeal ... *2 tbsp*
- Water ... *4 cups*
- Tomato puree ... *2 tbsp*
- Corn flour (if required) ... *1 tbsp*
- Butter ... *1 tbsp*
- Turmeric powder ... *½ tsp*
- Chilli powder ... *½ tsp*
- Sugar ... *1 tsp*
- Pepper powder ... *½ tsp*
- Salt ... *to taste*

  Baby Corn, thinly sliced for garnishing ...*4 nos*
- Parsley, chopped ... *2 tbsp*

Preparation and Cooking

1. Sear the skin of the tomatoes on the gas flame, peel and discard. Then chop them fine.
2. Heat butter and fry the cornmeal in it till golden.

3. Add chilli and turmeric powders; stir for a while and add chopped tomatoes.
4. Cook till tomatoes are limp; add tinned corn; stir and break the lumps.
5. Add water; bring it to boiling point and then simmer for 5 minutes.
6. Add tomato puree, corn kernels and salt in the soup.
7. Check the seasonings.
8. Add corn flour blended with 3 tbsp water and boil on high flame once again.

Serving

Garnish with sliced Baby Corn and Parsley and serve it hot. You may serve it with plain Popcorns, too.

Cooking time: 20 minutes.

2. Corn Dumplings Soup

- Cornmeal ... *½ cup*
- Flour ... *½ cup*
- Butter ... *1 tbsp*
- Water ... *1 cup*
- Corn cream-style/ Corn kernels, coarsely ground ... *½ cup*
- Onion, chopped ... *1 tbsp*
- Egg ... *1 no*
- Italian herbs ... *1 tsp*
- Ginger powder ... *¼ tsp*
- Pepper powder ... *½ tsp*
- Baking powder ... *½ tsp*
- Salt ... *1 tsp level*
- Stock, veg/non-veg... *5 cups*
- Cherry tomatoes... *12 nos*
- Parsley, chopped ... *2 tbsp*

Preparation and Cooking

1. Boil 1 cup water and add salt and baking powder.
2. Place cornmeal in a bowl and pour the hot water over it; stir till thick enough and cool.

3. Mix together flour, pepper powder, ginger powder and Italian herbs.
4. Add to the cornmeal mixture and mix well.
5. Beat one egg and pour into the cornmeal mixture.
6. Melt the butter and add it along with cream-style corn and chopped onion to the mixture.
7. Roll and shape into balls. Keep aside.
8. Boil veg or non-veg stock in the microwave for 10 minutes on High.
9. Check the seasonings and drop in the balls.
10. Cover the dish and cook for 8 minutes on High. Add cherry tomatoes in the soup and cook the dish for another 2 minutes.

Serving

Garnish with chopped Parsley and serve it hot with Chilli sauce.

Interesting Information

Dumplings are a favourite of the English and the American people, so they make a variety of them to add to their soup preparations.

Cooking time: 20 minutes.

3. Chinese Chicken Corn Soup

- Boneless Chicken breast ... *1 no*
- Corn cream-style ... *1½ cups*
  Or
- Tender Corn, grated ... *2 cups*
- Water/Chicken stock ... *6 cups*
- Eggs ... *2 nos*
- Corn flour ... *3 tbsp*
- Salt ... *to taste*

To serve with

- Soy sauce ... *2 tbsp*
- Green Chillies, chopped ... *3 nos*
- Table Vinegar ... *¼ cup*
- Chilli sauce ... *2 tbsp*

Preparation and Cooking

1. Put 5 cups chicken stock in a large deep micro-safe bowl; place corn and boneless chicken in it; cover with a lid and cook on High for 10 minutes in micro oven. Stand the dish for 5 minutes; open the lid and lift

chicken out of it; cool and cut it neatly into thin strips or shred it.

2. Keep the soup warm. Mix corn flour with remaining 1 cup stock and pour into the hot soup. Add 1 tsp salt and stir well. Cover and cook on micro High for 6 minutes or till it boils, stirring twice in between.
3. In the meantime, beat eggs and pour into the hot soup through a rice strainer (sieve with bigger holes) and keep stirring. Or pour the beaten eggs slowly from a height in a thin stream. Do not let the eggs form clots, so keep stirring with a fork.
4. Mix shredded chicken in the soup and heat through for 2 minutes on Reheat and serve.

Note: This soup is supposed to be of thick consistency, so if required you may increase quantity of corn flour.

This soup can be cooked without a microwave too, but you have to boil chicken beforehand and the same liquid can be used instead of water while preparing the soup.

Serving

Serve hot with Soy sauce, Chilli sauce and chopped chillies in Vinegar.

This is one of the most favourite Chinese soups liked by young and old alike in India and anywhere else.

Variation

Instead of chicken add 3 cups mixed Vegetables.

Tips

Do not add more salt to the soup because Soy sauce served along with it is very salty in nature.

Cooking time: 15 minutes for preparation and 18 minutes micro cooking.

4. Chicken, Shrimps, Sweet Corn Soup

- Sweet corn whole kernels ... *1½ cups*
- Shelled shrimps ... *¾ cup*
- Chicken breast, cut into cubes ... *1½ cups*
- Green Peas, shelled... *¾ cup*
- Chicken stock ... *4 cups*
- Tastemaker cube, Chicken ... *1 no*
- Corn flour ... *2 tbsp*
- Black Pepper powder... *1 tsp*
- Salt ... *to taste*

Preparation and Cooking

1. Place 3½ cups stock, chicken cube, corn kernels, shrimps, chicken and green peas in a large pan with a lid.
2. Bring to boiling point, cover and simmer for 5 minutes.
3. Mix corn flour with ½ cup remaining stock and add to the soup.

4. Cook, stirring all the time till soup thickens. Keep simmering for a while.
5. Season with salt and pepper.

Serving

Serve hot in soup bowls along with Soy sauce and Chilli sauce.

Tips

The Chinese are known to heat the serving plates and soup bowls before serving food in them.

This soup, too, is one of the popular soups enjoyed by young and old alike.

Cooking time: 10 minutes.

5. Corn and Mushroom Chowder

- Corn kernels ... *1½ cups*
- Mushroom, sliced... *1 cup*
- Red and Green Peppers ... *1 each, small*
- Tomato ... *1 large*
- Fish flakes (opt.) ... *1 cup*
- Spring Onions with greens ... *2 nos*
- Corn flour ... *3 tbsp*
- Parsley, chopped ... *1 tbsp*
- Stock ... *6 cups*
- Salt ... *to taste*

Preparation and Cooking

1. Cut peppers in juliennes and keep aside.
2. Blanch tomato, remove skin and cut into small pieces.
3. In a big micro-safe bowl combine stock, corn and mushrooms; cover and cook on High in micro oven for 10 minutes.

4. Mix corn flour with ½ cup water.
5. Add peppers, tomato, salt, fish and corn flour to the boiling soup; mix well and cook for 3 minutes on High, uncovered, stirring once.
6. Remove soup and check the seasonings.

Serving

Serve hot with Garlic bread.

Interesting Information

Chowder is a thick soup or a stew made of fish and various vegetables. Chowders are quite popular in the American continent.

Cooking time: 13 minutes micro cooking.

Salads

- Corn and Mushroom Salad
- Innovative Chicken-Corn Salad
- Tuna Fish and Corn Salad in Baked Spinach Ring
- Corn, Carrot, Cauliflower, and Coconut Salad
- Pungent Corn Salad
- Beetroot and Corn Salad

1. Corn and Mushroom Salad

- Corn kernels ... *1 cup*
- Mushrooms ... *200gm*
- Bean sprouts ... *½ cup*
- Spring Onions ... *3 nos*
- Cucumber ... *1 no, large*
- Tomatoes ... *2 nos*
- Cabbage leaves ... *6 nos*
- Lettuce ... *8 leaves*
- French Dressing ... *¼ -½ cup*

Preparation and Cooking

1. Remove the spine of cabbage leaves and 2 lettuce leaves. Roll them tightly and shred very fine. Immerse in cold water for 30 minutes to keep them crisp. Wash and immerse rest of the lettuce too.
2. Wash and steam corn kernels in the steaming basket with 2 tbsp water underneath, on micro High for 3 minutes. Remove and cool.

3. Wash and drain bean sprouts.
4. Cube 1 tomato and ½ cucumber.
5. Slice washed and cleaned mushrooms, spring onions, 1 tomato and remaining cucumber.
6. Place sliced mushrooms, steamed corn, bean sprouts, spring onions and cubed tomato and cucumber in a bowl; pour the French dressing over and toss; finally keep the mixed ingredients, covered, under refrigeration till used.
7. Drain the water from cabbage and lettuce and refrigerate. Assemble with mushroom mixture just before eating.

Serving

It is said that for assembling salads a **'careful carelessness'** should be applied.

Take a big platter; arrange the 6 lettuce leaves; spread the crisp cabbage leaves over it; form one circle of sliced tomatoes and another with sliced cucumber. Pile up mushroom mixture in the centre of lined platter and pour the leftover dressing on top. Serve the salad cold with any Indian or Continental meal.

Variation

- Instead of corn, use boiled Green Peas/cooked Beans in the salad.
- Add cooked and shredded Chicken or Chicken Salamis to the salad.
- Use French dressing without the addition of minced garlic in it.

Cooking time: 30 minutes for preparation and 3 minutes micro cooking.

2. Innovative Chicken-Corn Salad

- Corn kernels, boiled ... *1½ cups*
- Roasted Chicken, shredded ... *1½ cups*

  Or
- Tandoori Chicken pieces
- Potato, boiled and chopped ... *1 cup*
- Red Pepper, cut into cubes ... *½ no*
- Green Pepper, cut into cubes ... *½ no*
- Pickled Onions

  Or
- Shallots in Vinegar... *½ cup*
- Mustard sauce ... *¼ cup*
- Mayonnaise ... *¼ cup*
- Cream ... *½ cup*
- Peppercorns, crushed ... *10 nos*
- Rock Salt ... *to taste*
- Lettuce ... *8 leaves*
- Eggs, hard boiled, for garnishing ... *4 nos*

Preparation and Cooking

1. Combine red and green pepper cubes and cook them for 1 minute on micro High.
2. Mix together boiled potatoes, peppers, corn kernels, pickled onions and mustard sauce in a bowl and chill for 30 minutes or so.
3. Shred lettuce; immerse in cold water for 15 minutes and drain.
4. Combine shredded chicken, mayonnaise and cream lightly, and adjust salt.

Serving

Line a salad plate with shredded lettuce; then place chicken mayonnaise on it; finally top it with chilled corn and peppers coated with mustard sauce. Sprinkle crushed pepper on top of the salad. Garnish the salad platter with hard boiled egg slices and serve it immediately.

Cooking time: Preparation time 30 minutes and 10 minutes for assembling the salad.

3. Tuna Fish and Corn Salad in Baked Spinach Ring

- Tuna Fish, tinned... *100 gm*
- Corn kernels, steamed ... *200 gm*
- Green Pepper, chopped ... *½ no*
- Red Pepper, chopped ... *½ no*
- Spinach, chopped... *¼ cup*
- Pepper powder ... *1 tsp*
- Tomato sauce ... *¼ cup*
- Salt *to taste*
- Thick White sauce (opt.) ... *½ cup*

For Spinach Ring

- Spinach puree ... *2 cups*
- Potatoes, boiled, grated ... *2 nos, large*
- Fresh Breadcrumbs ... *3 slices*
- Cheese, grated ... *¼ cup*
- Butter ... *1 tbsp*
- Onion, chopped ... *1 no*
- Garlic, chopped ... *1 tbsp*
- Pepper powder ... *1½ tsp*
- Eggs ... *2 nos*
- Salt ... *to taste*
- Glass ring mould

Preparation and Cooking

1. Heat butter in a pan and sauté garlic and onion in it.
2. In a large bowl mix all the ingredients for spinach ring and add onion and garlic too.
3. Beat eggs and pour into the bowl of spinach ring ingredients. Mix well.
4. Grease properly the inside of glass ring mould with 1 tsp cooking oil.
5. Pour the mixture into it and cook in a microwave for first 10 minutes on Combination-1 mode; and then for 2 to 3 minutes on micro High.
6. Remove the dish and place it on the kitchen platform for cooling.
7. In the meantime, combine tinned tuna fish, corn, chopped peppers, spinach, tomato sauce, white sauce, salt and pepper, etc, in a bowl. Check the seasonings.

Serving

With the help of a spatula or palette knife un-mould the cooled Spinach ring in a serving plate and fill the centre with Tuna fish and Corn salad. Crisp toasts and a light Soup are the best accompaniments.

Variation

Fill any other salad in the centre of the spinach ring.

Tips

If you select Chilli Tuna fish for this salad, then you may reduce the quantity of pepper powder in it.

If you don't have a glass ring mould, you may use an aluminium cake ring mould for baking spinach ring; bake it in an electric oven or in cooking range for 30 minutes.

Cooking time: 20 minutes for preparation and 15 minutes for baking the ring. Cooling time is extra.

4. Corn, Carrot, Cauliflower, and Coconut Salad

- Corn kernels ... *1-1½ cups*
- Cauliflower, grated... *½ cup*
- Carrot, grated ... *½ cup*
- Cucumber, chopped... *1 no*
- Fresh Coconut, grated ... *1 cup*
- Coriander, chopped... *¼ cup*
- Green Chillies finely, chopped ... *2 nos*
- Spring Onion with greens, chopped ... *2 nos*
- Tomato, chopped ... *1 no*
- Lemon juice ... *2 tbsp*
- Cooking oil ... *1 tbsp*
- Mustard seeds ... *½ tsp*
- Asafoetida powder ... *½ tsp level*
- Pepper powder ... *½ tsp*
- Salt ... *to taste*
- Noodles, crisp fried ... *1 cup*
- Purple cabbage ... *to serve on*

Preparation and Cooking

1. Steam corn on micro High for 2 minutes and stand it for 3 minutes.

2. In the meantime, assemble all the chopped and grated ingredients in a big bowl.
3. Add steamed corn and mix it well. Cool.
4. Sprinkle lemon juice, salt and pepper over it just before serving.
5. Heat oil in a ladle, crackle mustard in it; add asafoetida and pour it over the salad.
6. Mix the salad lightly.

Serving

Transfer to a serving platter and sprinkle ½ cup crisp fried Noodles or grated and fried Potatoes over it. Serve it immediately with any meal, or serve this innovative salad in Cucumber boats or in empty shells of Tomatoes.

Cooking time: 20 minutes for preparation and 2 minutes for micro cooking.

5. Pungent Corn Salad

- Corn kernels ... *1½ cups*
- Radish, grated ... *1½ cups*
- Carrot, grated ... *1 no*
- Spring Onions ... *3 nos*
- Cucumber ... *1 no*
- Cherry Tomatoes ... *15-20 nos*
- Ajwain seeds ... *1 tsp*
- Fresh Ginger, grated ... *1 tbsp*
- Chilli-Garlic sauce... *1 tbsp*
- Pepper powder ... *1 tsp*
- Mayonnaise sauce... *¼ cup*
- Cooking Oil ... *1 tbsp*
- Salt ... *1½ tsp*
- Salad leaves ... *6 nos*

Preparation and Cooking

1. Wash and steam corn in a microwave for 2 minutes on High. Stand it for 2 minutes.
2. Squeeze grated radish and discard the liquid.
3. Cut spring onions into rings and cucumber into cubes.

4. Halve the cherry tomatoes.
5. Clean and finely shred salad leaves. Immerse in cold water for 30 minutes and drain.
6. Heat oil in a pan and crackle ajwain in it. Add grated radish and stir-fry for a while.
7. Sprinkle salt over it and cook for 2 to 3 minutes. Cool.
8. In a large bowl mix corn, carrot, radish, cucumber, onions, grated ginger, chilli-garlic sauce and pepper powder. Add mayonnaise and mix lightly. Cover and chill it nicely before serving.

Serving

Line a salad platter with shredded salad leaves. Mix halved cherry tomatoes with the chilled salad and pile it up in the centre of the platter. Serve with any Indian or Continental meal.

Tips

It is an innovative salad dish. Radish, ajwain, grated ginger and chilli-garlic make the salad pungent.

Cooking time: 15 minutes for preparation, 5 minutes cooking and 10 minutes for assembling.

6. Beetroot and Corn Salad

- Corn kernels ... *200 gm*
- Beetroot ... *2 nos*
- Green Chillies, chopped ... *2 nos*
- Coriander, chopped ... *¼ cup*
- Fresh Ginger, grated ... *1 tbsp*
- Pepper powder ... *1 tsp*
- Roasted Cumin powder ... *½ tsp*
- Cheese cream dressing ... *1 cup*
- Asafoetida powder... *½ tsp*
- Lettuce ... *1 head/8 leaves*
- Salt ... *to taste*

Preparation and Cooking

1. Clean and chop the lettuce very fine and immerse it in cold water.
2. Place corn in the steaming basket of a microwave and steam for 3 minutes on High. Stand for 3 minutes and then cool.

3. Cook beetroots too in the microwave for 3 minutes on High and cool.
4. Peel and grate beets with a thicker grater and cool, or chop them fine.
5. Mix green chillies, cumin, pepper, asafoetida and ginger with cheese cream dressing and chill it properly under refrigeration.
6. Drain water from the lettuce and line a shallow dish with it.

Note: In the absence of a microwave, corn and beets can be boiled traditionally in advance and cooled under refrigeration.

Serving

Mix corn with chilled cheese cream dressing and pile it up on the bed of lettuce. Place grated beet on top and sprinkle it with chopped coriander.

Serve it cold with any light meal, as corn itself is quite substantial.

It is an innovative salad dish.

Tips

Do not mix grated beet with dressing before serving, otherwise the salad will be coloured in sexy beetroot hues.

Cooking time: 8 minutes for cooking and 10 minutes for assembling it.

Snacks

- Makai Ghoogni
- Yummy Corn Balls
- Cornmeal Swirls
- Corn Pancakes
- Tacos
- Basic Tortillas and Enchiladas
- Cream Crackers topped with Chicken-Corn mixture

1. Makai Ghoogni

- Tender Corn kernels ... *200 gm*
- Potatoes Medium ... *4 nos*

  Or
- New Potatoes ... *500 gm*
- Curry leaves ... *2 sprigs*
- Coriander, chopped ... *¼ cup*
- Peppercorns, crushed ... *1 tbsp*
- Onion seeds/ Kalonji ... *1 tsp*
- Sugar ... *1 tsp*
- Pepper ... *a dash*
- Cooking Oil ... *50 ml*
- Salt ... *to taste*

Preparation and Cooking

1. Peel and cut potatoes into cubes and steam along with corn on micro High for 5 minutes. Let them stand for 2 minutes. Or steam new potatoes separately on High for 6 minutes, cool and peel.

2. Heat oil in a pan; add kalonji and peppercorns and cook for 30 seconds on high flame; add sugar, salt and curry leaves, stir and cook for 30 seconds more.
3. Now add steamed corn and potatoes; stir gently; cover and cook for 3 minutes on medium flame.

Serving

Garnish with chopped Coriander and serve it hot with Tomato Chutney/Sauce.

Interesting Information

This dish is a popular evening snack in Bengal. Earlier when fresh corn was in season, people used to boil the corn on cob and take out the kernels or the other way round, but now with availability of corn kernels (American/ Indian) everywhere, it is much easier to cook it.

Cooking time: 10 minutes for preparation and 10 minutes for cooking.

2. Yummy Corn Balls

- Cornmeal (Maize flour) ... *1 cup*
- Flour ... *¼ cup*
- Cheese, grated ... *¼ cup*
- Tender Corn, grated ... *½ cup*
- Milk ... *½ cup*
- Pepper powder ... *½ tsp*
- Chilli flakes ... *1 tsp*
- Italian herbs ... *1 tbsp*
- Baking Soda ... *¼ tsp*
- Oil ... *for frying*
- Salt ... *to taste*
- Cornflakes, crushed ... *to roll the balls*

Preparation and Cooking

1. Sift maize flour, salt, flour and baking soda in a bowl; mix in the milk and keep aside for 15 minutes.
2. In the meantime, heat oil to smoking point and lower the heat.

3. Add grated cheese, grated corn, Italian herbs, chilli flakes and pepper powder to maize flour mixture and mix it with a spoon vigorously for one minute.
4. Divide the mixture into equal sized portions. Roll each portion in the crushed cornflakes; drop in hot oil on medium flame and then increase the heat. Stir the balls gently and fry till light brown in colour.
5. Fry 5 to 6 balls only at a time. Remove them on absorbent kitchen paper.

Serving

Serve hot as a starter or as a snack with Tomato and Onion Chutney.

Tips

When tender corn on the cob is not available, ¼ cup corn kernels can be crushed and added to the maize flour to prepare this yummy snack.

Tomato and Onion Chutney: Cook together 1 cup chopped onions, 2 cups chopped tomatoes, 1" piece ginger, a few flakes of garlic and 4 green chillies finely chopped, in the microwave for 3 minutes, covered; or on the gas stove in the vegetables' own juices till they are limp. Cool for a while and grind to a fine paste.

Heat 1 tbsp oil and crackle ½ tsp cumin in it; add a pinch of asafoetida and pour over chutney. Serve at room temperature.

Variation: Mix maize flour, grated corn and mashed potato, season with herbs of your choice, shape into balls and deep fry.

Cooking time: 15 minutes for preparation and 20 minutes for frying.

3. Cornmeal Swirls

- Cornmeal/ Maize flour ... *1 cup*
- Rice flour ... *½ cup*
- Spinach puree ... *½ cup*
- Ginger powder ... *½ tsp*
- Ajwain ... *½ tsp*
- Red Chilli paste ... *1 tsp*
- Asafoetida powder... *½ tsp*
- Chilli powder ... *¼ tsp*
- Baking powder ... *¼ tsp*
- Cooking Oil ... *1 tbsp*
- Salt ... *to taste*
- Oil ... *for frying*

Kitchen press or Farsan-making machine to push the dough through it for making swirls

Preparation and Cooking

1. Sift together cornmeal, rice flour, salt, baking powder, chilli and ginger powders.
2. Mix together mashed spinach puree, sieved ingredients, ajwain, chilli paste and 1 tbsp oil properly and knead

it to a pliable dough. Keep it on the softer side and crack free.

3. Heat oil for frying to smoking point and then reduce the flame.
4. Divide the dough into 6 portions. Attach the disc with a star to the farsan-making machine and oil it from inside; put one portion of the dough in the cavity of the machine; replace the top portion of the machine and press them together.
5. Make swirls in the hot oil by pushing the dough through the gadget; increase the heat and fry the swirls till brownish and crisp from both sides.
6. Remove them with a slotted spoon and place on kitchen paper. Finish making swirls with all the dough.
7. Cool them properly and store in an airtight container.

Serving

Serve any time with Tea, Coffee or any other beverage. These swirls taste excellent with any Soup, too.

Tips

This is an innovative dish developed on the pattern of Chakli. Chakli is made of several flours; here I have used cornmeal as the main flour.

If, because of humidity, swirls seem a little soggy, heat them up either in a microwave for 1 to 1½ minute or in hot oven for 3 minutes and leave for a while.

Cooking time: 15 minutes for preparation and 30 to 35 minutes for frying.

4. Corn Pancakes

- Dosa Batter, well fermented ... *2 cups*
- Tender Corn, grated ... *1 cup*
- Asafoetida powder ... *¼ tsp*
- Salt ... *to taste*
- Coriander, chopped very fine ... *¼ cup*
- Green Chillies, chopped fine (opt.) ... *2 nos*
- Oil ... *for cooking*

Preparation and Cooking

1. Mix together dosa batter, grated corn, chopped coriander, chillies, salt and asafoetida. Add 1 tbsp oil in it and stir vigorously, and keep aside for 5 minutes.
2. Heat a non-stick pan. Smear it with a little oil and lower the heat.

3. Put 1 ladle full of the prepared batter; tilt the pan to spread it evenly and cook on high flame till pale brown. Add a few drops of oil on the edges and in the centre, and change the side of the pancake. Cook it from this side too till light brown and remove from the fire.
4. In this way make all the pancakes and store in a casserole to keep them warm.

Serving

Serve with Coconut chutney or Tomato chutney.

The recipe of Tomato Chutney has been given with 'Yummy Corn Balls'.

Tips

In the absence of tender corn, use frozen American corn kernels.

Grind ½ cup kernels to a coarse paste and add to the batter; the remaining ½ cup can be added in the form of whole kernels, and follow the same cooking instructions.

Cooking time: 15 minutes for preparation and 25 minutes for cooking pancakes.

5. Tacos

(Mexican Snack)

For Tacos

- Cornmeal/Maize flour ... *1 cup*
- Flour ... *¼ cup*
- Salt (opt.) ... *¼ tsp*

For Filling

- Tomatoes, finely chopped ... *2 nos*
- Lettuce, chopped ... *1 head/8 leaves*
- Celery, chopped ... *½ cup*
- Green Pepper, chopped ... *1 no*
- Spring Onions with greens, chopped ... *1 cup*
- Parsley, chopped ... *½ cup*
- Cheese, grated ... *1 cup*

Or

- Cooked stuffing of Kidney beans and Salad ingredients
- Enchilada sauce ... *to serve with*

Preparation and Cooking

1. Mix cornmeal, salt and flour together with water and prepare a soft dough. Divide it into 4 portions.
2. Roll out one portion into a thin disc, and with the help of a 2-3" biscuit cutter, take out as many discs as possible. Sprinkle some maize flour while rolling if required. Prick the discs with a fork lightly. In this way finish cutting and pricking all the discs; re-roll the leftovers of the dough and use it too.
3. Heat oil in a small frying pan; place the disc in medium hot oil, and with a pair of tongs fold it over to half; keep holding so that the edges do not touch each other till it is crisp; turn the side and then remove it on absorbent kitchen paper. Finish frying all the discs the same way.
4. Cool and store in an airtight container.

Serving

Fill each Taco with chopped salad; top it with Enchilada sauce and serve it immediately. Or place all the chopped ingredients, taco shells and hot (warmed up) Enchilada sauce on the table. Demonstrate how to fill a taco shell; and let all the family members or guests make their own tacos as per individual taste and enjoy them. Thus each one can relish this Mexican dish in his/her own way.

Taco is a tortilla folded into a turnover or rolled with filling and usually fried.

This Mexican cornmeal-flour based dish is eaten as a snack.

Important Information

These days readymade taco shells are available at grocery shops but they are quite small in size.

Recipe of Enchilada Sauce is given with 'Tortillas and Enchiladas'.

Cooking time: 15 minutes for preparation and 30 minutes for frying.

6. Basic Tortillas and Enchiladas

For Tortillas

- Cornmeal ... *1 cup*
- Flour ... *½ cup*
- Water/Buttermilk... *½ cup*
- Salt ... *¼ tsp*
- Water... *to knead soft dough*

For Enchilada Sauce

- Tomato sauce ... *1 cup*
- Water ... *2-2½ cups*
- Chilli powder ... *3 tbsp*
- Corn Oil/Oil ... *3 tbsp*
- Cornmeal ... *2 tbsp level*

For Stuffing

- Cheese, grated ... *2 cups*
- Spring Onions with greens, chopped ... *2 cups*

Preparation and Cooking for Basic Tortillas

1. Mix together cornmeal, flour, salt and water together to make soft dough.
2. Divide into 10-12 portions; roll into 6-7" discs.
3. Cook each disc on a hot griddle from both sides without applying any oil. Place in a casserole.
4. Finish rolling and cooking all the discs (tortillas).

Cooking for Enchilada Sauce

1. Heat oil for sauce and brown cornmeal slightly in it.
2. Add rest of the ingredients and cook for 10 minutes on medium fire, stirring constantly to avoid lumps.
3. Preheat the oven for moderate heat.

Assembly

Dip each tortilla in hot enchilada sauce and put it in a plate; spread the chopped onions and grated cheese on it. Roll the tortilla and place in a baking dish. Continue until all are rolled. Pour the remaining sauce over the enchiladas in the baking dish and sprinkle some more cheese over it. Heat in the hot oven till cheese melts.

Serving

Serve hot with tossed Green Salad and baked Beans.

Variation

La Casa Dia/Quesadilla: Place a cheese slice on one side of a basic tortilla and fold it into half. Oil a heavy non-stick pan lightly and heat it; place folded tortilla on it; keep turning it on low fire with a spatula until cheese inside is slightly melted and tortilla is warm enough. Serve. La Casa Dia can be eaten like a sandwich.

Tostada: Place a basic tortilla in a heavy non-stick pan that has been lightly oiled. Turn it over till thoroughly warm. Remove and place in a plate. Put ½ to 1-inch thick layer of cooked and mashed kidney beans or baked beans on tortilla, add finely chopped salad on top of it, sprinkle generous amount of grated cheese and finally top it with enchilada sauce. Serve immediately.

Important Information

Tortilla is a round, flat and unleavened bread made from cornmeal. It is one of the most important and the basic dish of Mexican cookery. Traditionally, many Mexican dishes are made from Corn and Cornmeal because it is the staple diet in Mexico.

7. Cream Crackers topped with Chicken-Corn mixture

- Cream Crackers ... *8 nos*
- Chicken, shredded ... *½ cup*
- Corn, grated ... *½ cup*
- Cheese, grated ... *¼ cup*
- Parsley, chopped ... *1 tbsp*
- Pepper powder ... *½ tsp*
- Cherry Tomatoes ... *8 nos*
- Green Pepper, chopped fine ... *½ no*
- Ginger powder ... *¼ tsp*
- Butter ... *1 tbsp*
- Egg (opt.) ... *1 no*
- Corn flour ... *1 tsp*
- Water ... *¼ cup*
- Salt ... *to taste*

Preparation and Cooking

1. Cook grated corn for 1½ minutes in microwave on High. Stand it for 2 minutes.
2. Heat butter in a pan; cook chopped green pepper in it till limp; add shredded chicken, cooked corn,

ginger and pepper powders, beaten egg, parsley and salt. Stir well.

3. Mix corn flour and water, and add to the mixture. Cook for a while and switch off the heat.
4. Sprinkle half of the cheese on it and mix. Cover and let it cool.
5. Cut cherry tomatoes into halves if they seem bigger.

Serving

Arrange cream crackers in a serving tray or any other fancy looking flat dish.

Spread the chicken-corn mixture on them with a butter knife; sprinkle cheese; top them with full or halved cherry tomatoes and serve immediately, lest the cream crackers become soggy.

Serve them with Tea/Coffee at mid-day or at teatime. They are ideal to be packed for small children's tiffin box.

Variation

Use freshly baked biscuits from Short crust pastry dough instead of cream crackers.

Instead of chicken, mix chopped and boiled Vegetables with corn. Or mix cooked and chopped Shrimps with corn and egg for topping the biscuits.

Tips

Topping mixture can be cooked and stored beforehand but while topping the biscuits it should be at room temperature. Mixture should be dry.

Cooking time: 5 minutes for cooking and 10 minutes for arranging and topping the biscuits.

Snacks

- Corn Stuffed Chilli Wada
- Cornflake Chewda
- Corn Fritters/Pakoda
- Steamed and Tossed Cornmeal Balls
- Popcorns
- Steamed Corn on the Cob
- Stir-fried Baby Corn Fingers
- Steamed Corn Cups

1. Corn Stuffed Chilli Wada

- Corn, grated and cooked ... *1 cup*
- Potato, large, boiled ...*2 nos*
- Cornmeal ... *½ cup*
- Mixed Spice powder ... *1 tsp*
- Mango powder/ Pomegranate powder ... *½ tsp*
- Chilli powder ... *1 tsp*
- Asafoetida powder... *¼ tsp*
- Big Green Chillies... *4 nos*
- Salt ... *to taste*

For Coating

- Gram flour ... *¼ cup*
- Maize flour ... *¼ cup*
- Ajwain ... *¼ tsp*
- Baking powder ... *¼ tsp*
- Water ... *to make batter*
- Salt ... *to taste*
- Oil ... *for frying*

Preparation and Cooking

1. Give a slit on one side of the chillies and remove the seeds.

2. Mix potato, corn, cornmeal and other ingredients for the stuffing; stuff the chillies with the mixture; cover them with rest of the corn-potato mixture and keep aside.
3. Mix all the ingredients for the batter; make batter of dropping consistency and keep aside for 15 minutes.
4. Heat oil in a frying pan to smoking point and then lower the heat.
5. Dip the stuffed chillies in batter one by one and deep fry on moderate heat till nice and crisp from all sides.
6. Take them out and place on absorbent kitchen paper.

Serving

Cut each Wada into two portions diagonally and serve with Tomato sauce. Or serve them with any meal as a side dish.

Cooking time: 25 minutes for preparation and 15 minutes for frying.

2. Cornflake Chewda

- Frying Cornflakes ... *1 cup*
- Peanuts, roasted ... *½ cup*
- Cashew nuts ... *¼ cup*
- Raisins ... *¼ cup*
- Curry leaves ... *¼ cup*
- Green Chillies, chopped (opt.) ... *4 nos*
- Murmura (puffed Rice) ... *2 cups*
- Gram flour Sevian... *1 cup*
- Salt ... *to taste*
- Turmeric powder ... *1 tsp*
- Chaat Masala ... *1 tsp*
- Mustard seeds ... *1 tbsp*
- Chilli powder ... *1 tsp*
- Sesame seeds (opt.) ... *¼ cup*
- Oil ... *for frying*

Preparation and Cooking

1. Heat oil to smoking point, lower the heat; add ¼ cup frying cornflakes in it; raise the heat; stir nicely and take out in a big strainer kept on a pan to drain excess oil. Finish frying all the cornflakes.

2. Place murmura in a large micro-safe dish and heat for 2 minutes on Reheat mode; or dry roast in a large pan for 10 minutes on low fire.
3. Heat 2 tbsp oil in a small pan and fry cashew nuts in it and remove; crackle mustard in the same oil; add green chillies and curry leaves and fry till crisp; add sesame seeds, turmeric and chilli powders, stir and remove from the fire.
4. In a large bowl/Parat, mix all the ingredients for Chewda; sprinkle salt and chaat masala; mix gently; cool and store in an airtight container.

Serving

Serve with Tea, Coffee or Cold drinks as a dry snack.

Tips

This dish has a shelf life of 10 to 15 days. In the humid areas if it loses crispness, heat in a microwave oven for 1 to 2 minutes (depends upon quantity).

Variation

Corn Chaat: Mix boiled and chopped Potatoes, boiled Corn, green Chutney, chopped Onion, Coriander and Tomato, Tamarind sauce or Tomato sauce, etc, with Chewda; and serve immediately as a snack.

Cooking time: 30 minutes.

3. Corn Fritters/Pakoda

- Baby Corn ... *20-24 nos*
- Oil ... *for frying*

For Batter

- Cornmeal/ Maize flour ... *½ cup*
- Gram flour ... *2 tbsp*
- Rice flour ... *2 tbsp*
- Corn flour ... *2 tbsp*
- Baking Soda ... *a pinch*
- Chilli-Garlic sauce... *1 tsp*
- Ajwain (opt.) ... *¼ tsp*
- Coriander seeds (opt.) ... *1 tsp*
- Coriander, chopped ... *2 tbsp*
- Salt ... *to taste*
- Water (add a little more water if required) ... *1 cup*

Preparation and Cooking

1. Wash and dry baby corn. Cut them lengthwise if the corncobs are thicker.
2. Sift all the flours, ajwain, baking soda and salt together in a bowl.

3. Add water; mix and make a smooth batter; cover and keep aside for 10 minutes.
4. Heat oil for frying in a pan; bring it to smoking point and then lower the heat.
5. Mix batter once again thoroughly; hold each baby corn from tail end; dip nicely in the batter; let the extra batter flow back into the bowl, and immediately put in the oil; increase heat and fry till nice and crisp. Place them on absorbent kitchen paper.
6. Fry three to four pieces at a time.

Serving

Serve hot with Chilli-Garlic sauce or Szechuan sauce as a snack or serve them with any light Soup.

Variation

Make batter the same way; add 1 cup Corn kernels, chopped Coriander and chopped green Chillies in it; put spoonfuls in hot oil and fry Pakodas the same way.

Tips

Standing the batter meant for frying for some time before use makes the fried product light in nature and it does not absorb extra oil.

Cooking time: 20 minutes for preparation and 15 minutes for frying.

4. Steamed and Tossed Cornmeal Balls

For Balls

- Corn kernels ... *1½ cups*
- Cornmeal ... *¼ cup*
- Paneer, grated ... *1 cup*
- Onion, chopped ... *2 tbsp*
- Green Chillies ... *3 nos*
- Garlic, chopped ... *1 tbsp*
- Ginger powder ... *½ tsp*
- Basil, dry ... *1 tsp*
- Mango powder ... *½ tsp*
- Salt ... *to taste*

For Tossing

- Cooking Oil/ Olive Oil ... *2 tbsp*
- Coriander/Fenugreek leaves, chopped ... *¼ cup*
- Tomato Sauce ... *¼ cup*
- Chilli-Garlic sauce... *2 tbsp*
- Soy sauce ... *1 tsp*

Preparation and Cooking

1. Wash and place fresh corn kernels, onion, garlic and green chillies in an electric grinder and make a smooth paste.

2. Mix together ground corn, cornmeal, grated paneer and all other dry ingredients.
3. Divide the dough into equal parts. Smear your hands with a little oil and roll each portion into a ball. You will get about 16 balls out of this recipe.
4. Place the rolled balls in the microwave steaming basket; put ¼ cup water underneath and steam them for 4 minutes on micro Medium.
5. Stand them for 5 minutes. Remove the basket and cool the balls. Store under refrigeration if cooked in advance.
6. Heat oil for tossing in a non-stick pan and fry coriander or fenugreek leaves in it.
7. Add all the other ingredients; mix and place the steamed balls in it and stir gently to coat evenly.

Serving

Serve on toothpicks with any sauce as Starters, or serve them with a Salad.

Variation

Place them in any Gravy of your choice and serve with Chapati or Phulka.

Cooking time: 20 minutes for preparation, 4 minutes for cooking and 4 minutes for tossing.

5. Popcorns

(Bhune Makki-ke-Dane)

- Popping corn (plain, not flavoured) ... *½ cup*
- Butter (opt.) ... *1 tbsp*
- Salt ... *to taste*

Cooking

1. Place popping corn in a brown paper bag and gently fold the mouth of the bag twice to close it lightly.
2. Roast on micro High for 2½ to 3 minutes or until popping begins to slow down.

Note: *Always roast popcorns in small quantity. Do not try popping corns in a low wattage microwave oven.*

Serving

Remove from the microwave, sprinkle a little salt and shake the bag; serve immediately.

Or transfer the popcorns to a bowl and pour some melted butter. Sprinkle a little salt; mix lightly to coat well and serve immediately.

Variation

Spicy hot Popcorn: Melt 2 tbsp Butter in a large bowl and add ¼ tsp Pepper powder and 3 drops of Tabasco or Capsico (hot Pepper sauce) in it. Place the freshly popped corn in it and stir until well coated. Serve them immediately.

Caramel Popcorns: Take ¼ cup melted Jaggery and ¼ tsp clarified Butter; heat up and pour over fresh unflavoured popcorns. Mix gently to coat evenly. Cool and serve.

Interesting Information

Plain or flavoured popcorns is one of the favourite snacks of young and old alike since time immemorial. It falls in the category of high protein, high fibre, low fat and low calorie energy food. These days you can't imagine a gathering, movie or home video viewing without the popcorns. In fact, nothing is easier than popping corn. Not only are the branded popcorns good, even the unbranded and American popping corn available loose is very easy to handle, with almost 95% success.

It is better to pop corn in a brown bag while cooking in the micro oven because the paper bag helps absorb moisture that would toughen the popped corn.

Popcorn is cooked in the bag with no butter or oil. As we all know that microwaves are attracted to moisture and there is enough moisture present in fresh popcorn to cook it, so, it is advisable to keep it fresh. Store the popping corn in a tightly sealed jar.

In North Indian villages, it is a common practice to caramelise roasted (in hot sand) corn and wheat grains and serve to the growing children as an evening snack. These **Bhune Dhane** are supposed to be very nutritious as they are full of protein and fibre.

We, as children, used to enjoy the treat on caramelised grains a lot whenever we visited our grandparents who, after my grandfather's retirement from a hi-fi service of the Indian Railways, settled down in a Punjab village to look after his vast lands. For us, a visit to them during summer vacations used to be a continuous picnic.

Tips

Those who do not own a microwave oven can also pop the branded or unbranded popping corn traditionally.

Place a heavy bottomed oiled vessel with a lid on high flame, heat it up and pour the corn in it, cover with a lid; within 5 minutes you will get the popcorns ready. This way, too, both the variations of popcorns can be tried and enjoyed.

Cooking time: 3 minutes in a microwave oven and 5 minutes on the traditional fire.

6. Steamed Corn on the Cob

- Corn on the cob ... *4 nos*

Preparation and Cooking

1. Clean corncobs. If too big, cut them into two. Steam on micro High for 5 minutes with ¼ cup water.

Serving Options

Corn on the Cob: Rub salt and lemon. Serve immediately.

Spicy Corn on the Cob: Cut into pieces, apply Tomato sauce/Chutney and serve.

Cheesy Corn: Cut into two lengthwise; arrange in a heatproof dish; sprinkle grated cheese, pepper powder evenly over them and grill for 5 minutes; serve hot.

Corn on the Cob Au Gratin: Brush with melted butter; roll in grated cheese and bake in hot oven for 10 minutes.

Cooking time: 5 minutes for steaming, 5 minutes for grilling, 10 minutes for baking.

7. Stir-fried Baby Corn Fingers

- Baby Corn ... *24 nos*
- Butter ... *3 tbsp*
  Or
- Olive Oil ... *2 tbsp*
- Chilli sauce ... *1 tbsp*
- Tomato puree (opt.) ... *¼ cup*
- Salt ... *to taste*
- Fresh Mint, chopped ... *2 tsp*

Preparation and Cooking

1. Wash and steam baby corns in microwave for 4 minutes on High. Stand them for 3 minutes.
2. Heat butter/oil in a pan; add fresh mint, tomato puree, chilli sauce and salt; stir properly and finally add steamed corn in it. Mix to coat evenly.

Serving

Garnish with Mint and serve hot as a starter.

Cooking time: 8 minutes.

8. Steamed Corn Cups

- Corn kernels, steamed ... *3 cups*
- Butter (opt.) ... *2 tbsp*
- Rock Salt powder ... *1 tsp*
- Pepper ... *1 tsp*
- Chilli powder ... *1 tsp*
- Mango powder ... *1 tsp*
- Mint powder/ Chaat Masala ... *1 tsp*
- Salt ... *to taste*

Preparation and Cooking

1. Heat butter in a deep pan, mix boiled corn in it and sauté.
2. Add rest of the ingredients in it and mix thoroughly.

Serving

Serve it hot in individual bowls or paper cups as a snack.

Variation

Add different seasonings to the steamed corn to get various flavours.

Interesting Information

This type of preparation of steamed corn is very popular with the younger generation in India. These days all the shopping malls have outlets selling this and college-going youth and other shoppers enjoy it any time of the day.

Cooking time: 5 minutes for heating up cooked corn and another 3 minutes for mixing it.

Main Course

Side Dishes

- Bhutta Salan
- Corn Koftas in Rajasthani Gravy
- Corn Upma
- Corn and Spinach Delight
- Okra, Baby Corn, Shallots and Cherry Tomatoes Surprise
- Corn on Eggplant Roundels

1. Bhutta Salan

(Corn Curry)

- Corn on cob ... *3 nos*
- Coconut, grated ... *1 no*
- Coriander, chopped ... *1-1½ cups*
- Green Chillies ... *4 nos*
- Onion, chopped ... *1 no*
- Ginger-Garlic paste... *1 tbsp*
- Corn flour ... *1 tbsp*
- Salt ... *to taste*

Tempering

- Cooking Oil ... *2 tsp*
- Red Chillies, whole... *2 nos*
- Mustard seeds ... *½ tsp*
- Curry leaves (opt.)... *1 sprig*

Preparation and Cooking

1. Heat 1 cup water for 1 minute on micro High and soak grated coconut in it. Grind together grated coconut with its water, green chillies, coriander, onion and ginger-garlic paste; strain through a sieve and take out first extract of thick herbal coconut milk. Add another cup of warm water and repeat grinding process and

collect second extract of coconut milk. Discard the coconut remaining.

2. Clean and wash corn on cob and cut each into 3 to 4 pieces; place them in the steaming basket and steam for 3 minutes on micro High. Keep them aside, covered.
3. In a big micro-safe bowl mix together coconut milk, 1 cup water, corn flour and salt and cook on High for 7 minutes, uncovered, stirring once in between. The mixture should come to boiling point.
4. Place boiled corn pieces in the hot coconut milk; cover and cook for 12 minutes on Medium. Stand the dish for 5 minutes.
5. Heat oil in a ladle on top of the gas stove; crackle mustard in it; add whole red chillies and curry leaves; switch off the gas and pour the tempering over corn curry. Adjust the salt.

Serving

Serve hot with Rice preparation/Chapati or Khakhra, etc.

Tips

This dish is supposed to have thin coconut curry; it will thicken slightly once it cools down. The fun is in eating the dish. You are supposed to eat the corn dipping the pieces in curry repeatedly and suck out the curry and corn juices. You'll love it once you start eating it. The dish becomes a favourite with young and old alike, even your guests start enjoying it, so you may have to cook it often, as is the case in my house. You may increase or decrease the number of chillies used in the recipe according to taste.

Note: If you want to use readymade coconut milk, then omit the grated coconut. Grind all other ingredients with 1 cup water; squeeze the green juices, mix with readymade coconut milk and follow the recipe.

Cooking time: 22 minutes micro cooking.

2. Corn Koftas in Rajasthani Gravy

For Koftas

- Tender Corn on Cob ... *2 nos*
- Cottage Cheese ... *¾ cup*
- Gram flour ... *¼ cup*
- Green Chillies ... *2 nos*
- Coriander, chopped... *¼ cup*
- Mixed Spice powder ... *1 tsp*
- Red Chilli powder (opt.) ... *1 tsp*
- Salt ... *to taste*
- Oil ... *for frying*

For Rajasthani Gravy

- Tomato puree ... *2 cups*
- Chilli-Garlic sauce... *½ cup*
- Butter ... *¼ cup*
- Ajwain ... *1 tsp*
- Basil, chopped ... *1 tbsp*
- Cream (opt.) ... *¼ cup*
- Sugar ... *1 tsp*
- Mixed Spice powder ... *1 tsp*
- Coriander, chopped ... *¼ cup*

Preparation and Cooking

1. Grate corn, and mix with crumbled cottage cheese and all the other ingredients for koftas except oil for frying. Do not add water. Mix well and divide into 12-14 equal portions; roll into balls and keep aside. Harder corn can be steamed and grated.
2. Heat oil for frying to smoking point; lower the heat and then fry 2-3 koftas at a time on medium flame till light brown in colour. Remove and place them on kitchen paper; or place the rolled koftas in the steaming basket and steam on micro High for 3 minutes; stand them for 3 minutes and then place in the gravy immediately. This way you can avoid frying.
3. Heat butter for gravy and crackle ajwain in it.
4. Add tomato puree and cook for 3 minutes.
5. Put chilli-garlic sauce and half the chopped coriander in tomato puree and cook till oil separates.
6. Add 2 cups of water; boil for 3 minutes and then simmer the gravy for 10 minutes; add sugar, salt, mixed spice, basil and cream, and check the seasonings.

Serving

Place the koftas in a shallow serving dish; heat gravy and pour over them; garnish with remaining Coriander and serve the dish hot with Boiled Rice or Rajasthani 'Do Palli-Ki-Roti' or hot Phulkas.

Tips

Always place soft koftas in the gravy just before serving, otherwise they will absorb the gravy and will be too soft to handle. Heat koftas separately before putting in the gravy if fried much earlier, but not with gravy unless mentioned in the recipe.

Cooking time: 15 minutes for preparation and 30 minutes for cooking.

3. Corn Upma

- Fresh Corn/Corn kernels ... *2 cups*
- Onion, chopped ... *1 no*
- Green Chillies, chopped ... *2 nos*
- Curry leaves ... *1 sprig*
- Semolina ... *2 tbsp*
- Peanut powder ... *¼ cup*
- Turmeric ... *1 tsp*
- Mustard seeds ... *1 tsp*
- Sugar ... *1 tsp*
- Mixed Spice powder ... *1 tsp*
- Lemon juice ... *1 tbsp*
- Asafoetida powder... *¼ tsp*
- Cooking Oil ... *3 tbsp*
- Tomato, chopped (optional) ... *1 no*
- Carrot, grated ... *¼ cup*
- Green Peas, boiled... *¼ cup*
- Coriander, chopped ... *¼ cup*

Preparation and Cooking

1. Steam corn in microwave on High for 2 minutes; cool and grind 1½ cups coarsely and keep ½ cup as kernels.

2. Heat oil in a large non-stick pan and crackle mustard in it.
3. Add curry leaves, chopped green chillies and onion and fry for 2 minutes or till transparent.
4. Add corn and fry for 2 minutes.
5. Put semolina, peanut powder, asafoetida and turmeric; fry for 1 minute and sprinkle salt over it.
6. Add ¼ cup water, chopped tomato, green peas and grated carrot; cover the pan with a lid; cook on slow flame for 6 minutes or cook in a microwave for 3 minutes on High and let it stand for 3 minutes.
7. Mix with a fork and sprinkle lemon juice over it.
8. Add half the chopped coriander and mix lightly.
9. Transfer to a serving dish and sprinkle rest of the coriander.

Serving

Serve hot with Tomato Sauce or Mint Chutney.

Cooking time: 10 minutes for preparation and 10 to 12 minutes for cooking.

4. Corn and Spinach Delight

- Corn kernels ... *1½ cups*
- Spinach puree ... *2 cups*
- Cashew paste ... *¼ cup*
- Milk ... *½ cup*
- Fresh Cream (opt.) ... *¼ cup*
- Garlic, chopped ... *2 tbsp*
- Cumin ... *½ tsp*
- Pepper powder ... *1 tsp*
- Mixed Spice powder ... *¼ tsp*
- Salt ... *to taste*
- Cooking Oil ... *2 tbsp*

Preparation and Cooking

1. Heat oil in a pan, fry garlic in it till pink and remove.
2. Crackle cumin in the same oil; add spinach and fry; add cashew paste, salt, pepper and milk; and cook for 5 minutes on medium flame.
3. In the meantime, steam corn kernels on micro High for 3 minutes and stand.

4. Add corn to the spinach and cook for 3 minutes; add cream and mix well.
5. Transfer spinach and corn to the serving dish and garnish it with fried garlic.
6. Heat 1 tsp oil; add a dash of red chilli powder to it and finally pour it over the corn-spinach preparation.

Serving

Serve it hot with Makki-ki-Roti or toasted Brown Bread slices and a thin Clear Soup.

Spinach puree: Cook washed and roughly chopped spinach on high flame with ½ cup water, uncovered; cool and pass through a mixer. If required add ¼ cup milk while grinding it.

Cooking time: 15 minutes for preparation and 14 minutes for cooking.

5. Okra, Baby Corn, Shallots and Cherry Tomatoes Surprise

- Okra/Ladyfingers, (small sized) ... *300 gm*
- Baby Corn ... *200 gm*
- Shallots/Madras Onions ... *½ cup*
- Cherry Tomatoes ... *½ cup*
- Chilli flakes ... *1 tsp*
- Pepper powder ... *½ tsp*
- Lemon juice ... *1 tbsp*
- Olive Oil ... *2-3 tbsp*
- Maize flour (opt.) ... *1 tbsp*
- Salt ... *to taste*

Preparation and Cooking

1. Wash and clean the ladyfingers; remove the heads and give a long slit on one side.
2. Wash and steam baby corn for 2 minutes in a microwave on High. Keep aside, covered.

3. Mix 1 tsp salt and pepper powder and sparingly fill in the slits of ladyfingers with the help of a butter knife.
4. Heat olive oil in a non-stick pan; add shallots and stir-fry on high flame for 2 minutes or till pinkish in colour.
5. Add ladyfingers and stir-fry; sprinkle with lemon juice; cover and cook for 3 minutes.
6. Open the lid; put in corn and cherry tomatoes and continue cooking.
7. Remove from fire and dish out in a flat serving dish.

Serving

Serve hot with plain Paratha and a Rayita, or as a side dish with Dal and Rice, or serve it as a side dish with any Continental meal.

Variation

Use thickly sliced Ladyfingers (deep-fried) and steamed Corn kernels instead of whole ladyfingers and baby corn; decrease the quantity of Olive oil to 1½ tbsp and sprinkle Pepper powder and Lemon juice along with Salt and Chilli flakes.

Tips

You may use any other combination of spices according to your family's taste.

Cooking time: 15 minutes for preparation and 10 minutes for cooking.

6. Corn on Eggplant Roundels

- Eggplant ... *1 large*
- Corn cream-style ... *2 cups*
- Onion-Tomato paste ... *1½ cups*
- Egg (opt.) ... *1 no*
- Cheese, grated, for each roundel ... *1 tbsp*
- Turmeric ... *1 tsp*
- Chilli powder ... *1 tsp*
- All Spice powder ... *1 tsp*
- Ginger-Garlic paste ... *1 tbsp*
- Oil ... *1 tbsp*
- Ajwain ... *½ tsp*
- Parsley, chopped ... *2 tbsp*
- Salt ... *to taste*
- Oil ... *for frying*

Preparation and Cooking

1. Cut eggplant into ½-inch thick roundels; prick them with a fork; sprinkle salt over them and keep aside.
2. Heat oil and crackle ajwain in it; add ginger-garlic paste and sauté; sprinkle all the dry ingredients and mix well, add onion and tomato paste and fry well.

3. Mix cream-style corn and half the parsley in it. Cook till all the moisture evaporates. Cool. Beat egg lightly and mix with the tomato and corn mixture.
4. Heat oil in a deep frying pan and fry the eggplant roundels in it. Shake them before frying.

   Or steam the roundels for 3 minutes in a microwave on High. Cool and remove.
5. Take a large oven proof flat or shallow dish and arrange the fried eggplant roundels in it. Spoon the tomato-corn mixture on each roundel and spread to cover it. Cover all the roundels this way.
6. Sprinkle 1 tbsp grated cheese on each roundel and cook in a hot oven till cheese melts.

Serving

Garnish the dish with chopped Parsley and serve it hot with Chapaties or Phulkas.

Variation

You may mix 200 gm cooked Mutton mince with corn and tomato mixture and follow rest of the recipe.

Tips

Avoid cutting eggplant with iron knife as the roundels will turn black. Use a knife with a steel blade.

Cooking time: 35 minutes.

Main Course

Roties and Pulao

- Moughlai Roti with Corn Stuffing
- Corn and Baby Corn Pulao
- Corn Methauries with Orange Rayita
- Basket of Makki-ki-Roties
- Corn Bread (American Style)

1. Moughlai Roti with Corn Stuffing

For Roties

- Wheat flour ... *¼ cup*
- Cornmeal ... *¼ cup*
- Refined flour ... *¼ cup*
- Semolina ... *¼ cup*
- Curds ... *¼ cup*
- Salt ... *½ tsp*

Sift together all the flours and salt; use curds and water to make a soft and pliable dough; cover and keep aside for 30 minutes. In the meantime prepare the stuffing.

For Stuffing

- Fresh Corn, grated... *1 cup*
- Carrot, grated ... *½ cup*
- Spring Onion, chopped ... *½ cup*
- Green Pepper, chopped ... *½ no*
- Coriander, chopped ... *¼ cup*
- Chilli sauce ... *1 tbsp*
- Cooking Oil ... *¼ cup*
- Eggs ... *3-4 nos*
- Cheese, grated ... *½ cup*
- Seasonings ... *to taste*
- A few paper napkins

Preparation and Cooking

1. Heat 1 tbsp oil in a pan and stir-fry chopped onions for 1 minute.
2. Add corn and cook for 2 minutes, stirring all the time.
3. Add pepper and carrot; stir for a while and add chilli sauce and other seasonings. Break one egg and mix it with corn stuffing for binding. Cover and keep aside.
4. Once again knead the dough for Roti and divide it into equal sized portions.
5. Heat a tava/griddle or a non-stick pan.
6. Roll each portion of dough into a 6-7" disc and cook it on tava from both the sides.
7. Finish cooking all the rolled discs (roties) this way and keep them covered and warm.
8. Beat rest of the eggs in a shallow dish and keep aside.
9. Finally, pour a few drops of oil on the non-stick tava/ griddle; heat it up and lower the heat; soak one roti at a time in beaten egg and place it on hot griddle; cook it from both the sides, using a little oil.
10. Sprinkle some grated cheese and chopped coriander; place 1 tbsp heaped corn and vegetable stuffing in the centre of the roti and fold it from both the sides. Wrap a paper napkin folded in half around it and serve.

Serving

Serve hot with Green chutney, Tomato sauce and finely sliced Salad as a snack or a light meal.

Variation

Use cooked and shredded Chicken or Minced meat along with corn as a stuffing.

Tips

You may use leftovers of Tandoori or Roasted Chicken shreds for stuffing.

Cooking time: 10 minutes for making dough; 10 minutes for making stuffing and 30 minutes for cooking roties and assembling.

2. Corn and Baby Corn Pulao

- Basmati Rice ... *1½ cups*
- Corn kernels ... *1½ cups*
- Baby Corn ... *15 nos*
- Brown Onion ... *1 tbsp*
- Red Chillies, whole... *2 nos*
- Ginger powder ... *1 tsp*
- Red Pepper flakes... *2 tbsp*
- Turmeric ... *1 tsp*
- Tomato puree ... *¼ cup*
- Italian herbs ... *1 tsp*
- Lemon juice ... *1 tbsp*
- Cooking Oil ... *3 tbsp*
- Salt & Pepper ... *to taste*
- Water/Stock ... *3 cups*
- Parsley, chopped ... *2 tbsp*

Preparation and Cooking

1. Wash and soak rice for 30 minutes.
2. Mix oil and whole red chillies in a micro-safe bowl with a lid and heat on High for 2 minutes, uncovered.

3. Add corn kernels along with baby corns, Italian herbs, salt, turmeric and ginger powder; mix well and add tomato puree; cover and cook for 3 minutes on High.
4. Mix rice, lemon juice, red pepper flakes, brown onion and water; stir and cook on High for 10 minutes, covered.
5. Stir again lightly and cook for 10 minutes on Medium, covered.
6. Stand the dish for 5 minutes before serving.

Serving

Garnish the cooked corn rice with chopped Parsley and additional Pepper flakes; loosen the rice slightly with a fork and serve the dish hot with cool Carrot Rayita.

Carrot Rayita: Beat 2 cups fresh curds with salt, pepper, a pinch each of asafoetida and ginger powder and cool. Grate carrots and steam in a microwave for 1½ minutes; cool and put into the curds. Garnish with chopped coriander.

Cooking time: 33 minutes micro cooking.

3. Corn Methauries with Orange Rayita

For Methauries

- Cornmeal/ Maize flour ... *2 cups*
- Fenugreek leaves, cooked, chopped ... *1¼ cups*
- Cottage cheese, grated ... *1 cup*
- Ajwain ... *½ tsp*
- Baking Soda ... *a pinch*
- Green Chilli paste ... *1 tsp*
- Garlic paste ... *1 tsp*
- Ginger powder ... *½ tsp*
- Salt ... *to taste*
- Oil ... *for frying*

For Orange Rayita

- Fresh Curds ... *3 cups*
- Oranges ... *4 nos*
- Sugar, powdered ... *3 tbsp*
- Cardamom powder ... *½ tsp*
- Pepper powder ... *1 tsp*
- Salt ... *to taste*

Preparation and Cooking

1. Beat curds along with pepper, cardamom and sugar powders and keep it under refrigeration for cooling.

2. Peel oranges; clean; remove the piths and cut the segments into small pieces. Add oranges and salt to the curds; mix well and keep rayita under refrigeration till required.
3. Mix together cornmeal, chopped fenugreek leaves, grated cottage cheese, ajwain, baking soda, chilli and garlic pastes and salt.
4. Knead well and divide the dough into 20 equal portions.
5. Roll each portion on a folded kitchen napkin into a 4-5" disc. Sprinkle a little cornmeal on the napkin while rolling. Finish rolling all the methauries.
6. Heat oil for frying to smoking point and lower the heat.
7. Put one rolled disc at a time in the oil; increase the heat and turn once, so that it puffs well and gets evenly crisp. Remove and place on absorbent kitchen paper.
8. Finish frying all methauries and serve them hot.

Serving

Serve with Orange Rayita for breakfast or as a holiday special brunch or lunch.

Variation

If you and your family members do not relish fried items for any reason, cook the rolled Methauries on a hot griddle from both sides and serve.

Interesting Information

A 16th century work lists foods of the Gangetic plains of Uttar Pradesh and Bihar; and 'Methauri' is one of the popular fried preparations. Here, from a single line description in the food history, I developed this classic dish into an innovative one with cornmeal, fenugreek leaves and paneer into the Poories.

Cooking time: 20 minutes for preparation and 15 to 20 minutes for frying.

4. Basket of Makki-ki-Roties

Basic dough for plain Makki-ki-Roti:

- Cornmeal ... *3 cups*
- Ghee/Oil ... *for frying or applying on top*
- Water/ Buttermilk ... *2¼ cups*

Preparation and Cooking

1. Place 2½ cups cornmeal in a large shallow bowl or 'Parat' and make a well in the centre.
2. Add water or buttermilk, half at a time and start mixing with your hands; keep sprinkling rest of the liquid till all the cornmeal is assembled into a ball and turned into a soft dough. Divide the dough into 8 equal sized balls.
3. Heat a tava/griddle or a heavy bottomed non-stick pan.
4. Take a big kitchen cloth napkin and fold it twice to get a square and sprinkle some dry cornmeal on it.

5. Moisten your hands with a little water; take one portion of dough and flatten it like a patty. Place it on the folded napkin and start patting to flatten it into a 6-inch disc; keep sprinkling a little more cornmeal and changing the side of the disc while flattening it.
6. Take the disc on your palm and place it on the hot griddle to cook from both sides. Apply a little oil all over the half done cornmeal Roti on both the sides and cook to your satisfaction.

   Or dry roast half done Roti directly on the gas flame, changing sides time to time with a pair of tongs. You may apply butter or clarified butter on it.
7. Finish cooking all the cornmeal Roties this way and place them in a casserole on a clean folded napkin and cover with a lid.

Note: Makki-ki-Roties are slightly coarse in comparison to wheat Chapaties/Phulkas. They turn softer when kept covered in a casserole.

Serving

Serve with Sarson-ka-Saag, homemade white Butter and Curds or with any other Veg or Non-veg curried dish.

Variations

Kuddhoo/Choori: Turn 1 Roti into bread-like crumbs; add 1½ tbsp melted Ghee or Butter and 2 tbsp sugar or ¼ cup grated Jaggery to it; turn into a coarse ball and then eat it as a dessert or as a breakfast dish.

Makki-ki-Methiwali Roti: Add 2 cups fresh Fenugreek leaves sautéd in 1 tbsp oil, 2 tsp Salt, 1 tsp green Chilli paste, ½ tsp Ajwain seeds and ½ tsp Ginger powder to the basic cornmeal dough. Cook as for plain roti.

You may fry the Methi Roti by applying oil to the half done roties or dry roast them directly on the gas flame.

Makki-ka-Aloo Paratha: Add 3 mashed Potatoes, ¼ cup chopped Coriander, 3 chopped green Chillies, ½ tsp Ginger powder, 1 tsp Pomegranate seeds powder, ½ tsp Ajwain, ½ tsp mixed Spice powder, some Salt to the basic Cornmeal dough. Cook as plain roti, dry or fried.

Makki-ka-Gobi Paratha: Take 2 cups grated Cauliflower, cook in a microwave for 2 minutes on High, covered, and add to the basic cornmeal dough. Add the same condiments as for Makki-ka-Aaloo Paratha.

Makki-ka-Mooli Paratha: Take 2 cups Cornmeal, 2 cups grated Radish and a few of its leaves finely chopped, 1 tsp Ajwain, 1 tsp Chilli powder, 1 tsp Mango powder, ½ tsp Ginger powder and Salt to taste; add as much water or Buttermilk as required to make a soft and pliable dough. Follow the same procedure for cooking as for other Roties.

Note: You may cook grated radish for 2 minutes before adding to cornmeal.

Makki-ka-Hara Paratha: Take 2 cups Cornmeal, 2 cups Spinach puree, 1 tbsp green Chilli paste, 1 tsp Ginger powder and Salt in a big bowl, add as much water as required to make soft pliable dough. Make half done roties and fry them with a little oil on hot tava.

Take **any leftover vegetables**, puree them and mix with the cornmeal, season it well and make Roties for breakfast.

Important Note: Cornmeal dough should not be made in advance. Mix it with any of the above mentioned vegetables as and when required, and as much as required, just before making roties.

Cornmeal itself does not have long shelf life. Therefore, whenever you buy it, finish within 15 to 20 days.

Interesting Information

Many people in Indian villages turn the roties into coarse crumbs, put in the seasoned curds and gulp it down with buttermilk. In such cases, Roties are cooked in advance.

Sarson leaves and Corn mainly grow in the winter months in North India, that is why this combination is relished at that time of the year, whereas in Western India, Corn grows almost throughout the year, so people here enjoy Makki-ki-Roti as 'Bhakri'. They mix cornmeal with fenugreek leaves and make Roties out of it.

Cooking time: 20 minutes.

5.Corn Bread (American Style)

- Cornmeal ... *500 gm*
- Wheat flour/ Maida ... *250 gm*
- Sugar ... *4 tbsp*
- Baking powder ...*1½ tbsp*
- Eggs ... *4 nos*
- Milk ... *2¼ cups*
- Double Cream ... *½ cup*
- Butter ... *½ cup*
- Salt ... *1½ tsp*

Preparation and Cooking

1. Mix together cornmeal, wheat flour, sugar, baking powder, butter and salt in a bowl.
2. Separate egg whites and yolks, and blend egg yolks with milk and mix with the ingredients in a bowl.
3. Add double cream and just stir it. Beat egg whites very stiff and fold into the mixture in the bowl.
4. Pour into well-buttered muffin pans, filling them three-quarters full and bake in the hot oven for 30-35 minutes. Serve immediately.

Cooking time: 20 minutes for preparation and 35 minutes for baking.

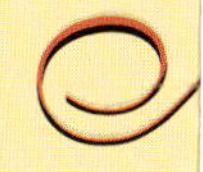

1. Polenta

(Sauted Corn Mush)

- Yellow Cornmeal ... *1 cup*
- Water ... *4 cups*
- Salt ... *1 tsp*
- Italian herbs ... *2 tsp*
- Butter ... *2 tbsp*
- Grated Cheese ... *½ cup*
- Tomato sauce/Meat and Tomato sauce ... *1½ cups*

Preparation and Cooking

1. Sift cornmeal and salt together; combine with 1 cup water.
2. Heat remaining water to boiling point.
3. Gradually add cornmeal mixture into the boiled water. Add salt, Italian herbs and 2 tbsp butter in it.
4. Place in a micro-safe bowl. Cook for 5 minutes on High in a microwave oven. Take it out and stir properly.

5. Cover and cook again on High for 5 minutes. Stand for 5 minutes in oven.
6. Remove and serve it hot with sauce or meat sauce.

Note: Is delicious to be eaten like this.

Variations

- Add grated cheese to the mixture and pour it into a greased baking dish, sprinkle with a little more cheese and bake in moderately hot oven until brown.
- Pour into greased mould; cover and chill until firm. Cut into slices and serve with any of the sauces.
- Cut into ½-inch thick slices; coat with cornmeal and shallow fry in hot fat, turning to brown on both sides.

Serving

Serve shallow fried pieces with Sauce or Honey or Corn syrup or even Maple syrup.

Tips

- Especially in Italian cookery, 'Polenta' is a breakfast dish but I feel that it can also be served as part of any main meal.
- In American cookery, the same dish is known as Corn Mush or Sautéd Corn Mush.

Cooking time: 10 minutes for preparation and 10 minutes micro cooking.

2. Corn and Vegetable Soufflé

- Fresh Corn kernels, cooked/Canned Corn kernels ... *1 cup*
- Cheese, grated ... *½ cup*
- Mixed Vegetables, finely chopped ... *1 cup*
- Eggs ... *2 nos*

For White Sauce

- Milk ... *2 cups*
- Butter ... *2 tbsp*
- Flour ... *2 tbsp*
- Salt ... *1 tsp*
- Peppercorns, freshly pounded ... *1 tsp*

Preparation and Cooking

White Sauce

1. Heat butter in a micro-safe bowl for 1 minute.
2. Add flour; stir and cook on micro High for 1 minute, uncovered. Add milk and stir.
3. Put a lid and cook on micro High i.e.100 % power for first 2 minutes, stirring once and then on Medium for 5 minutes, stirring twice in between with a hand beater/ egg-beater.
4. Take out the dish and smell it. If a nice aroma of cooked flour is spreading around, that means the sauce is ready, otherwise cook it for 1 minute more on micro High and let the dish stand for a couple of minutes, covered, to avoid any formation of film on top.
5. Remove the lid and add salt and crushed peppercorns.

Note: To make a nice and smooth sauce, it is important that all the ingredients are at room temperature; how you are cooking it (in microwave or traditional way on gas heat, etc) is immaterial.

However, if while cooking lumps are formed, pass the sauce through a liquidizer and then through a sieve. Sprinkle a little more milk and mix. Keep it covered until used.

Soufflé

1. Place mixed vegetables in the steaming basket and cook on micro High for 2 minutes. Stand them for 3 minutes.
2. Preheat the electric oven or cooking range for moderate heat.
3. Separate egg yolks and whites.
4. Beat egg yolks. Mix beaten yolks, corn, vegetables and grated cheese with white sauce.
5. Beat egg whites stiff but not dry, and fold in.
6. Pour the mixture into a greased ovenproof dish and bake in a moderately hot oven for 30 to 35 minutes.

Serving

Serve immediately with toasted Bread and a good Soup.

Tips

As a rule of thumb, baked Soufflés are served hot, immediately after they are baked.

Cooking time: 11 minutes micro cooking and 30 minutes baking.

3. Baby Corn Pizza

(Italian Bread)

- Pizza shells ... *4 nos*
- Capsicums, thinly sliced ... *½ cup*
- Black Olives, halved ...*8 nos*
- Baby Corn, halved ... *12 nos*

  Or
- Corn kernels, boiled...*½ cup*
- Mozzarella Cheese, grated ... *1½ cups*
- Pizza sauce ... *1½ cups*

For Pizza Sauce

- Onion-Tomato paste...*1 cup*
- Tomato puree ... *1 cup*
- Chilli-Garlic sauce...*1 tbsp*
- Butter ... *1 tsp*
- Oregano ... *2 tsp*
- Pepper powder ... *2 tsp*
- Ajwain ... *1 tsp*
- Sugar ... *1 tsp*
- Capsicum, finely chopped ...*¼ cup*
- Chilli powder (opt.) ...*1 tsp*
- Parsley, chopped ... *2 tbsp*
- Bay leaf ... *1 no*
- Salt ... *to taste*

Preparation and Cooking

1. Heat butter in a pan and add ajwain (carom seeds) to crackle. Add chopped capsicum and cook for 1 minute on high flame.
2. Now add all the other ingredients for pizza sauce to it except parsley. Mix well and cover with the lid. Cook for 3 minutes and remove the dish. Take out the bay leaf and sprinkle chopped parsley.
3. Preheat the Convection mode of your microwave oven for 15 minutes on 200 degrees Celsius or any electric oven or oven of a cooking range for 20 minutes.

Assembly

Apply pizza sauce generously on pizza shells. Sprinkle some cheese over them; arrange sliced vegetables or meats artistically and finally top with grated cheese. Cover the shell nicely from all sides.

Baking

Bake pizzas in hot oven one by one for 10 minutes or till cheese melts.

If you own a cooking range, 3 to 4 pizzas can be baked at a time.

Serving

Cut the prepared Pizza into wedges and serve hot with Mustard/Tomato Sauce as a starter or as part of the meal with Soup, Salad and any of the Italian or Continental baked dishes.

Tips

If your microwave has no Convection mode, then first crisp one side of the pizza shell under the grill for 2 to 3 minutes, then apply pizza sauce and veggies/meats and finally grill each shell for 5 minutes or till cheese melts. Repeat the cooking process with rest of the shells.

Note: Prepared Pizza can be reheated very well in the micro mode. Place 1 full pizza of room temperature on a paper plate or kitchen paper towel and Reheat on High for 1½ to 2 minutes.

Avoid

Having too much of pizzas without salad or soups. Enjoy junk food as a mini meal and cultivate a habit of consuming nutritious soups and salads along, as a healthy diet should include fibrous food like vegetables, fruits and dry fruits along with other food items.

Interesting information

"The name Pizza originated from the area around Naples in southwest Italy. It is not certain, however, that the nearby village of Pizza, where the flour for the best pizza dough is grown and ground, can claim to be its creator. A pizza may first have been made to use up left-over bread dough and tomato sauce, plus whatever sausage, ham or cheese happened to be available" says the **Cordon Bleu** book on '**Cheese and Savouries**'.

Cooking time: 10 minutes for cooking pizza sauce and 10 minutes each for baking pizzas.

4. Corn Pudding

- Corn cream-style ...2½ *cups*
- Eggs ... *2 nos*
- Milk ... *2 cups*
- Soft Breadcrumbs... *1 cup*
- Cheese, grated ... *¼ cup*
- Parsley, dried ... *¼ tsp*
- Salt & Pepper ... *to taste*

Preparation and Cooking:

1. Beat eggs and milk together.
2. Add breadcrumbs and corn. Mix well.
3. Add grated cheese and stir.
4. Season it with salt and pepper and sprinkle parsley.
5. Pour in a greased dish and cover with cling film.
6. Half fill a large bowl with water; boil on micro High for 8 minutes; place the pudding bowl in it and cook on micro Medium for 15 minutes.
7. Let the dish stand for 5 minutes and then remove.

Serving

Serve hot with toasted Bread or any Continental meal.

Variation

Mix 50% Corn and 50% Vegetables and follow the recipe.

Tips

- You can steam Corn Pudding in a pressure cooker or in a traditional electric oven too.
- But in any case you should place the pudding bowl in another vessel half filled with water.
- In traditional cooking methods, pudding will take 30 to 35 minutes to cook.

Cooking time: 10 minutes for preparation and 23 minutes micro cooking.

5. Meatless Corn Pie

- Flour ... *½ cup*
- Cornmeal ... *1 cup*
- Chilli powder ... *1½ tsp*
- Salt ... *2 tsp*
- Pepper ... *¼ tsp*
- Baking powder ... *¼ tsp*
- Corn cream-style... *3 cups*
- Tomato sauce ... *½ cup*
- Milk ... *1 cup*
- Butter/Oil ... *½ cup*
- Eggs ... *3 nos*
- Onion, grated ... *¼ cup*
- Black Olives/ Mixed Vegetables, chopped ... *1 cup*

Preparation and Cooking

1. Preheat the oven for moderate heat.
2. Beat eggs.
3. Sift together flour, cornmeal, salt, chilli, pepper and baking powder.

4. Combine cream-style corn, tomato sauce, milk, fat and eggs, and stir.
5. Blend dry ingredients into corn mixture and mix well.
6. Add grated onion and black olives or mixed vegetables.
7. Grease a large ovenproof dish and pour the mixture into it.
8. Spread it properly and bake in a moderately hot oven for 1 to 1½ hours.

Serving

Serve hot with any Sauce as a main meal with some light Soup and Salad.

Cooking time: 15 minutes for preparation and 1½ hours for baking.

6. Baked Beans and Corn Bake

- Corn, grated ... *2 cups*
- Baked Beans (tinned) ... *2 cups*
- Chicken Sausages, skinless ... *4 nos*

  Or
- Chicken mince, cooked ... *1 cup*
- White sauce ... *2 cups*
- Cheese, grated ... *½ cup*
- Ginger, fresh ... *1" piece*
- Pepper powder ... *1 tsp*
- Green pepper ... *½ no*
- Tomato, thinly sliced ... *1 no*
- Salt ... *to taste*

Preparation and Cooking

1. Place grated corn in a micro-safe bowl and cook it covered for 2 minutes on micro High.
2. Slice sausages thinly.
3. Chop green pepper and ginger very fine.

4. Mix together cooked corn, baked beans, sausages or minced meat, chopped pepper, salt, ginger and pepper powder.
5. Mix white sauce and half of the grated cheese with the corn mixture.
6. Transfer the mixture to a micro-safe or ovenproof dish.
7. Arrange the sliced tomatoes on top and sprinkle rest of the cheese.
8. Either cook in a micro oven for 10 minutes on Combination -1 mode or bake in a moderately hot oven for 20 minutes or till the cheese melts.

Serving

Serve hot with Garlic bread or crisp Toasts and a light Soup.

Cooking time: 20 minutes.

7. Corn Patties Baked

- Corn kernels ... *250 gm*
- Potatoes, boiled ... *4 no*
- Cheese, grated ... *¼ cup*
- Fresh Breadcrumbs... *1 cup*
- Coriander, chopped ... *¼ cup*
- Green Chilli paste ... *1 tsp*
- Ginger, grated ... *2 tbsp*
- Pepper powder... *2 tsp level*
- Pomegranate seeds ... *1 tbsp*
- Butter ... *1 tbsp*
- Salt ... *to taste*

Preparation and Cooking

1. Wash and boil corn with ½ cup water; or micro cook for 3 minutes on High with ¼ cup water, covered. Cool and grind it coarsely.
2. Mash potatoes well.
3. Roast and powder pomegranate seeds.
4. Preheat your electric oven for moderate heat.
5. Mix together mashed potatoes, corn, breadcrumbs, cheese, butter, ginger, coriander, chilli paste, pomegranate seeds powder, salt and pepper. Knead well.
6. Smear your palms with a little oil and divide the dough into 12 to 14 equal sized portions.
7. Flatten each portion and give it a desired shape; finish shaping all the portions and place them in a non-stick baking tray or an aluminium baking tray lined with foil.
8. Bake the patties for 40 to 45 minutes; remove and serve them hot.

Serving

Serve hot with Tomato sauce and Coleslaw.

Cooking time: 15 minutes for preparation and 40 minutes for baking.

8. Chilli Corn A La Crème

- Corn kernels, whole ... *1½ cups*
- Fresh Cream ... *½ cup*
- Chilli flakes ... *1 tsp*
  Or
- Red Chilli powder ... *½ tsp*

Preparation and Cooking

1. Combine fresh corn kernels and salt and cook in microwave on High for 3 minutes, covered. Add less salt if using canned corn kernels.
2. Mix together cooked kernels and cream. Add chilli powder at this stage if using.
3. Place in a micro-safe glass bowl. Sprinkle with chilli flakes, cover and heat through on Reheat mode of micro oven for 2-3 minutes.

Serving

Serve hot with Garlic bread or any other bread well toasted.

Cooking time: 6 minutes micro cooking.

Main Course

Non-vegetarian

- Bhutta-N-Keema
- Baby Corn and Chicken in Chilli-Garlic Sauce
- Fish Monte Carlo
- Prawns and Baby Corn
- Mutton Mince and Corn Rava (Dalia)
- Fish and Corn Cutlets With Corn Sauce
- Two-crust Chicken, Corn and Vegetable Pie

1. Bhutta-N-Keema

(Baby corn and Mutton mince)

- Baby Corn ... *200 gm*
- Mutton/Chicken mince *250 gm*
- Onion-Tomato paste ...*½ cup*
- Tomato puree ... *½ cup*
- Ginger, grated (opt.)...*1 tsp*
- Mixed Spice powder...*1 tsp*
- Chilli powder ... *1 tsp*
- Turmeric powder (optional) ... *1 tsp*
- Cumin ... *½ tsp*
- Nutmeg powder... *a pinch*
- Coriander, chopped ... *¼ cup*
- Cooking Oil ... *2 tbsp*
- Thick Coconut milk...*½ cup*
- Salt ... *to taste*

Preparation and Cooking:

1. In a micro-safe bowl put oil and cumin and cook on micro High for 2 minutes, uncovered.

2. Place minced meat in the same bowl and cook on High for 3 minutes, covered, stirring once in between. Remove and loosen it with a fork and cook for another 3 minutes, uncovered.
3. In the meantime wash baby corn and steam with ½ tsp salt sprinkled over it on High for 3 minutes.
4. Mix onion-tomato paste, tomato puree, grated ginger, chilli and turmeric powder, mixed spice, baby corn and half of the coriander with meat mince thoroughly.
5. Add ½ to 1 cup water; adjust salt; cover the dish and cook on micro High for 10 minutes.
6. Remove from the oven and let it stand for 3 minutes.
7. Open the dish; sprinkle nutmeg and add thick coconut milk.

Serving

Garnish the dish with rest of the Coriander and serve with hot Chapaties/Parathas or Buns.

Variation

Instead of corn, use 200 gm cubed Potatoes.

Cooking time: 20 minutes micro cooking.

2. Baby Corn and Chicken in Chilli-Garlic Sauce

- Baby Corn ... *250 gm*
- Chicken breast ... *1 no*
- Chilli-Garlic sauce... *½ cup*
- Tomato puree ... *½ cup*
- Spring Onions with greens ... *4 nos*
- Vinegar ... *¼ cup*
- Corn flour ... *¼ cup*
- Egg ... *1 no*
- Chicken stock ... *1½ cups*
- Oil ... *for frying*
- Salt ... *to taste*
- Parsley, chopped ... *1 tbsp*

Preparation and Cooking

1. Cut chicken breast into 1-inch squares or thin strips and marinate with vinegar, salt and 1 tbsp chilli sauce for 2 hours.
2. Clean and finely chop spring onion with greens.

3. Heat oil for frying.
4. Sprinkle corn flour over the marinated chicken pieces (saving 1 tsp for thickening the gravy); add beaten egg and mix them well; deep fry in moderately hot oil and place on kitchen paper.
5. Heat 1 tbsp oil and sauté chopped spring onions in it. Wash baby corns and sauté in the same oil.
6. Add tomato puree; chilli-garlic sauce, 1½ cups chicken stock and salt.
7. Boil the stock and the baby corns for 3 minutes on high flame. Add chicken pieces and simmer it.
8. Mix 1 tsp corn flour with 3 tbsp water and pour it into the simmering gravy. Boil for a minute or two and then remove.

Serving

Garnish with chopped Parsley and serve it hot with steamed or Veg fried Rice.

Cooking time: 2 hrs and 10 minutes for preparation and 25 minutes for cooking.

3. Fish Monte Carlo

- White sauce ... *2 cups*
- White Fish, cooked and flaked ... *1½ cups*
- Sweet corn cream-style ... *1 cup*
- Corn kernels ... *½ cup*
- Eggs ... *2 nos*
- Cheese, grated ... *½ cup*
- Fresh Breadcrumbs... *½ cup*
- Butter ... *1 tsp*
- Bacon rashers (optional) ... *4-5 nos*

Preparation and Cooking

1. Preheat the electric oven for moderate heat.
2. Mix together white sauce, sweet corn cream-style and corn kernels.
3. Separate egg yolks and whites. Add yolks to the sauce and mix.
4. Beat egg whites stiff and fold into the sauce.

5. Add grated cheese (saving a little for the top) to the sauce mixture and mix lightly.
6. Grease an ovenproof dish, fill by layering the sauce and fish together, finishing with the sauce.
7. Mix crumbs and butter together with your fingertips and sprinkle over the sauce.
8. Finally sprinkle the dish with remaining cheese and bake in moderately hot oven for 20 to 30 minutes.

Note: You may place the dish in microwave and cook on Combination-1 mode for 15 minutes.

Serving

For serving, grill the Bacon rashers and place them on top of the dish and serve this French delicacy hot with Tomato sauce and crisp Toasts.

Tips

The recipe for White sauce has been given with 'Corn and Vegetable Soufflé'.

Cooking time: 15 minutes for preparation and 30 minutes for baking.

4. Prawns and Baby Corn

- Prawns ... *200 gm*
- Baby Corn ... *300 gm*
- Celery, chopped fine ... *¼ cup*
- Red Pepper, chopped fine ... *¼ cup*
- Vinegar ... *¼ cup*
- Corn flour ... *1 tbsp*
- Pepper powder ... *1 tsp*
- Salt ... *to taste*
- Cooking Oil ... *3 tbsp*
- Water ... *1 cup*

Preparation and Cooking

1. Marinate prawns in vinegar and salt; keep aside for 30 minutes and drain.
2. In the meantime steam corn in the microwave for 3 minutes.
3. Heat oil in an open pan; sauté prawns in it and lift out.

4. Add corn and celery, and cook for 2 minutes, stirring gently.
5. Mix prawns with corn and celery.
6. Add water, salt and pepper, and let it boil for 2 minutes.
7. Mix corn flour with a little water and thicken the dish.
8. Sprinkle red pepper and remove.

Serving

Serve with any meal as a side dish.

Cooking time: 30 minutes for preparation and 10 minutes for cooking.

5. Mutton Mince and Corn Rava (Dalia)

(Roughly ground dry Corn kernels and minced Meat)

- Mutton mince ... *200 gm*
- Corn rava ... *1 cup*
- Red Pepper ... *½ no*
- Yellow Pepper ... *½ no*
- Red Chillies, whole...*2 nos*
- Cashew nuts ... *15 nos*
- Onion, finely chopped ... *1 no*
- Green Chilli, finely chopped ... *1 no*
- Tomato puree ... *½ cup*
- Ginger powder ... *1 tsp*
- Clove powder ... *1 tsp*
- Mustard seeds ... *½ tsp*
- Cooking Oil ... *3 tbsp*
- Coriander, chopped ... *2 tbsp*
- Water/Mutton Stock ... *3½ cups*
- Salt ... *to taste*

Preparation and Cooking

1. Place corn rava in an envelope and roast in microwave on High for 2 minutes. Shake once in between. Or dry roast it in a pan/kadai.
2. Heat oil in a pan/kadai and lower the heat. Fry cashew nuts in it to a golden colour and remove.
3. Crackle mustard in the same oil; add whole red chillies, chopped onion and green chilli in it; and cook till pinkish in colour.
4. Add minced meat in it and cook for 5 minutes, stirring all the while to avoid lumps.
5. Sprinkle salt, clove and ginger powders; add tomato puree and mix well.
6. Sprinkle roasted corn rava on it and keep stirring.
7. Add water or stock and check the salt.
8. Chop half the cashew nuts and add to the mixture. Stir.
9. Transfer corn and minced meat mixture into a big micro-safe bowl; cover it with a lid or cling wrap and cook it for first 10 minutes on micro High and then for next 5 minutes on micro Medium; stirring once in between. Let the dish stand for 5 minutes. Stir it with a fork and garnish. If cling wrap is used, pierce it with a knife or fork in the centre of the dish.

Serving

Garnish with remaining Cashew nuts and chopped Coriander, and serve it hot as a breakfast dish. Green Chutney and Tomato sauce are the best accompaniments.

Variation

Cook the Corn rava with finely chopped and partially steamed Vegetables and Moong sprouts instead of minced mutton/chicken. Use Buttermilk instead of water, and juice of 1 Lemon instead of tomato puree. Rest follow the same procedure.

Cooking time: 25 minutes.

6. Fish and Corn Cutlets With Corn Sauce

For Cutlets

- Fleshy Fish with centre bone ... *500 gm*
- Tender Corn on cob ... *4 nos*
- Green Chillies, chopped ... *3 nos*
- Coriander, chopped ... *¼ cup*
- Mango powder ... *1 tsp*
- All Spice powder ... *1 tsp*
- Red Chilli powder ... *1 tsp*
- Rock Salt powder ... *1 tsp*
- Salt ... *1 tsp*
- Corn flour ... *2 tbsp*
- Egg ... *1 no*
- Oil ... *for frying*

For Corn Sauce

- Butter ... *2 tbsp*
- Onion, chopped fine ... *1 large*
- Garlic, chopped ... *1 tbsp*
- Red Chilli, whole ... *2 nos*
- Tomato puree ... *½ cup*
- Fresh Corn, grated ... *½ cup*
- Ajinomoto ... *¼ tsp*
- Water/Veg stock ... *2½ cups*
- Red Chilli powder ... *1 tsp*
- Ginger powder ... *½ tsp*
- Pepper powder ... *½ tsp*
- Salt ... *to taste*
- Sugar (opt.) ... *1 tsp*
- Corn flour ... *1 tbsp*

Preparation and Cooking

1. Wash and steam fish for 5 minutes in a microwave on High. Cool and remove the skin and bones. Or steam fish traditionally on gas stove heat.
2. Grate corn on the cob and steam it separately with ¼ cup water for 3 minutes on micro High. Cool.
3. Mix steamed corn, fish and all other dry ingredients for cutlet. Mash the mixture properly.
4. Divide it into 4 or 8 parts and shape each portion. Pat with a little cornmeal and keep aside.
5. Heat oil and fry these fish and corn cutlets in it. Remove and place on kitchen paper.

Corn Sauce

Deseed the whole red chillies. Heat butter in a pan; add red chillies, chopped onion and garlic and sauté. Sprinkle corn flour and stir till it turns pinkish. Add water, salt, pepper, chilli powder, ajinomoto and ginger powder. Bring it to boiling point and add tomato puree and ½ cup steamed corn. Mix it properly and simmer till the sauce is well blended and of pouring consistency. If need be, add ¼ cup boiled water in it to make it of pouring consistency. Garnish it with Parsley. Cover it and keep it warm.

Serving

Place one cutlet in each serving plate with some crisp salad and serve it along with prepared Corn Sauce with any Continental meal, or as you like.

Variation

Vegetarian gourmets may replace fish with boiled Potato and go ahead with the rest of the recipe.

Cooking time: 30 minutes.

7. Two-crust Chicken, Corn and Vegetable Pie

For Plain Pastry (two-crust pastry)

- Flour ... *2 cups*
- Salt ... *1 tsp*
- Butter ... *2/3 cup*
- Water, chilled ... *5-6 tbsp*

Sift flour and salt together. Add butter to flour and mix it with your fingertips till it resembles bread crumbs.

Now add cold water to hold ingredients together. Sprinkle a little more cold water evenly and form a ball. Divide the mixture into two portions.

For Stuffing

- Corn, boiled ... *1 cup*
- Mushrooms, sliced ... *¼ cup*
- Green Peas, boiled ... *¼ cup*
- Capsicum, chopped ... *¼ cup*
- Chicken, boiled, cooked, diced ... *1 cup*
- White sauce ... *1½ cups*
- Cream ... *½ cup*
- Egg yolk *1 no*
- Butter *2 tbsp*
- Red Pepper, chopped ... *2 tbsp*
- Basil, chopped ... *2 tsp*
- Salt & Pepper ... *to taste*

Preparation and Cooking

1. Brown mushrooms and capsicums in butter.
2. Mix cream, green peas, white sauce, chicken, salt, pepper, etc.
3. Heat over hot water. Beat egg yolk and add to the chicken mixture.
4. Heat stirring constantly for 1 minute. Keep aside.
5. Preheat oven for moderate heat.
6. Roll out one portion of the dough in a circular shape on a lightly floured board.
7. Pie should be about 1/8-inch thick. Fit loosely into 8 or 9-inch pie shell. Gently pat out the air pockets.

Trim pastry to 1-inch of edge of pie pan/shell; fold underneath.

8. Roll out the second portion also in the same way.
9. Fill the pastry with the filling. Cut slits in the second circle of pastry to allow steam to escape; place over filling; fold edge of top pastry under lower pastry to form a standing rim.
10. Pinch pastry edges or press with a fork.
11. Bake it in a moderately hot oven for 25-30 minutes.

Serving

Serve the baked pie hot as a main meal with some light Soup.

Cooking time: 20 minutes for preparation and 30 minutes for baking.

Sweet Treats

- Cornflake Bars
- Corn Hulwa
- Cornmeal Muffins
- Cornflake Cookies
- Corn and Coconut Cake with Custard Sauce

1. Cornflake Bars

- Cornflakes ... *1½ cups*
- Eggs ... *2 nos*
- Sugar ... *1 cup*
- Walnut kernels ... *1 cup*
  Or
- Almonds ... *¾ cup*
- Flour ... *¾ cup*
- Butter ... *½ cup*
- Baking powder ... *1 tsp*
- Salt ... *½ tsp*
- Orange Rind, grated ... *½ tsp*

Preparation and Cooking

1. Sift together flour, salt and baking powder.
2. Preheat the electric oven for moderate heat.
3. Coarsely grind walnuts and cornflakes.
4. Beat eggs and add sugar.
5. Cook over hot water, stirring constantly, for almost 10 minutes.

6. Add butter and beat well. Add rind and cool.
7. Add cornflakes, sifted flour and chopped walnuts, and mix well.
8. Put in a lined and greased cake tin or spread in an 8" x 8" ovenproof greased dish and bake in a moderately hot oven for 20 minutes.
9. Cool and cut into bars.

Serving

Serve at teatime as a snack.

Cooking time: 10 minutes for preparation and 35 minutes for cooking.

2. Corn Hulwa

- Corn kernels ... *1 cup*
- Sugar ... *¼ cup*
- Clarified Butter/ Ghee ... *¼ cup*
- Jaggery, grated ... *¼ cup*
- Milk ... *1 cup*
- Green Cardamoms... *4 nos*
- Mixed Nuts ... *¼ cup*

Preparation and Cooking

1. Steam corn kernels in the microwave steaming basket for 3 minutes on High; cool; place in electric grinder and grind coarsely.
2. Take out seeds of cardamoms and pound them.
3. Chop nuts of your choice finely.
4. Heat ghee in a non-stick pan; add corn and fry on medium flame for 5 minutes or till it turns pinkish.

5. Add milk; stir and cover it with a lid, and cook till the milk dries up (about 5 minutes on medium fire).
6. Add sugar, grated jaggery and pounded cardamom seeds. Fry till sugar is well blended and hulwa is dry and turns into a mass.

Serving

Garnish with chopped Nuts and serve it hot or at room temperature as a dessert.

Tips

You can grate fresh tender corn on cob also to make this dish.

This delicious dish is one of the favourites of my aunt Ms Dubey, who stays in Nagpur.

Cooking time: 5 minutes for preparation and 15 minutes for cooking.

3. Cornmeal Muffins

◆ Cornmeal	... *1½ cups*	◆ Butter	... *¼ cup*
◆ Corn flour	... *¼ cup*	◆ Baking powder	... *1 tsp*
◆ Jaggery syrup	... *¼ cup*	◆ Baking Soda	... *1 tsp*
Or		◆ Eggs, large	... *2 nos*
◆ Honey	... *2 tbsp*	◆ Milk	... *1 cup*
		◆ Clove powder	... *1 tsp*

Preparation and Cooking

1. Sift together cornmeal, corn flour, clove powder, baking powder and baking soda.
2. Heat milk; mix with cornmeal and keep aside.
3. Preheat electric oven for moderate heat.
4. Break eggs; mix one by one with cornmeal mixture and beat well after each addition.

5. Melt butter and pour in the mixture and mix well.
6. Warm jaggery syrup and add this too to the cornmeal. Or add honey and beat well.
7. Now pour this mixture into the muffin plate and bake for 20-25 minutes.
8. Remove and serve hot or invert them on wire rack, cool and store.

Note: The muffin batter will be of pouring consistency, so fill the muffin cups three-fourths only.

Serving

Serve at teatime.

Cooking time: 15 minutes for preparation and 20 minutes baking.

4. Cornflake Cookies

◆ Cornflakes	... *2½ cups*	◆ Black Raisins	... *2/3 cup*
◆ Flour	... *1 cup*	◆ Baking powder	... *1 tsp*
◆ Butter	... *½ cup*	◆ Egg	... *1 no*
◆ Sugar	... *1/3 cup*		

Preparation and Cooking

1. Crush cornflakes and clean sultanas.
2. Preheat the electric oven for moderate heat.
3. Cream butter and sugar until light and fluffy.
4. Break egg; beat it and mix with fluffy butter and sugar.
5. Sift flour and baking powder together and fold into the mixture.
6. Add crushed cornflakes and sultanas and mix lightly.

7. Divide into equal size portions.
8. Lightly roll each portion on your palm and press it slightly.
9. Finish rolling all the portions; place them on lightly greased oven trays allowing room for spreading; bake them in a moderately hot oven for 20 minutes.

Note: This quantity of mixture will yield 25-30 cookies. When cool, store them in an airtight jar.

Serving

Serve with tea/coffee at mid-day or teatime. They are ideal to be packed in small children's tiffin box, too.

Cooking time: 15 minutes for preparation and 20 minutes for baking.

5. Corn and Coconut Cake with Custard Sauce

◆ Cornmeal	... *1 cup*	◆ Eggs	... *2 nos*
◆ Corn flour	... *¼ cup*	◆ Desiccated Coconut	... *½ cup*
◆ Butter	... *¼ cup*	◆ Baking Soda	... *1½ tsp*
◆ Sugar	... *½ cup*	◆ Baking powder	... *¼ tsp*
◆ Milk	... *1 cup*		

Preparation and Cooking

1. Sift cornmeal, corn flour, baking powder and baking soda together in a bowl.
2. Heat milk and mix it with cornmeal mixture properly and keep aside.
3. Preheat an electric oven for moderate heat.
4. Prepare a ring mould for baking the cake.
5. Beat eggs and sugar together on a pan of hot water till sugar is dissolved.

6. Melt butter and mix it with egg and sugar mixture.
7. Pour sugar and butter contents in cornmeal bowl a little at a time and mix.
8. When sugar, butter and egg mixture is nicely mixed, then add desiccated coconut and lemon juice. Mix once again.
9. Pour the mixture in the ring mould and bake in the centre of the oven for 30-35 minutes.

   Note: If your baking mould is not heavy, then place additional aluminium plate under the mould.

10. Remove cake from the oven and invert it on the wire rack; let it cool for 10 minutes; with the help of a butter knife loosen the cake from the mould and take it out onto a plate.

Serving

Slice and serve with tea, coffee or any other beverage. You may even serve the sliced cake with hot Custard sauce as a dessert. Place 2 cake roundels in a quarter plate; pour 2 ladles of hot custard over them and serve immediately.

Custard Sauce: Boil 500 ml Milk with 2 tbsp Sugar in it. Blend 2 tbsp Custard powder with ¼ cup Milk and pour into the hot milk, bring it to boiling point; simmer for a minute or two and then remove. Add 2 tbsp chopped Nuts and ¼ tsp green Cardamom powder in it.

Cooking time: 15 minutes for preparation and 30 minutes for baking.

Dressings for Salads

- Mayonnaise
- Mustard Sauce
- Cheese Cream Dressing
- Simple French Dressing

1. Mayonnaise

- Egg Yolks ... *2 nos*
- Salt ... *2 tsp*
- Mustard powder ... *1 tsp*
- Vinegar ... *3 tbsp*
- Sugar ... *1 tsp*
- White Pepper Powder ... *1 tsp*
- Vegetable Oil ... *1½ cups*

Preparation

1. Combine egg yolks, salt, sugar and pepper in a blender or a processor and mix on slow speed.
2. Add vinegar and oil alternately, drop by drop, when processor is running.
3. Continue adding just a few drops of oil and vinegar at a time till an emulsion has formed; then keep adding 1 tbsp oil at a time and processing until thick, creamy.
4. Add mustard powder and pepper; churn once to mix well and store under refrigeration. Use as required.

This recipe will give you approximately 2 cups Sauce.

Note: Mayonnaise can be stored under refrigeration for more than 2 months. It can be used as a dressing for Salads and as a spread for Sandwiches.

Variation

Use of Whole egg, Lemon juice instead of vinegar and a little less oil is good for immediate use.

Tips

If by any chance your mayonnaise sauce separates while making, combine 1 egg yolk and a pinch of dry mustard in the processor bowl and process. Add the curdled mayonnaise to the egg, spoon by spoon, and process till the curdled sauce is smooth again.

Preparation time: 15 to 20 minutes.

2. Mustard Sauce

- Dry Mustard Powder ... *25 gm/¼ cup*
- White Bread, crust-less ... *2 small slices*
- Vinegar ... *½ cup*
- Sugar ... *1 tsp*
- Salt ... *2 tsp*

Preparation

1. Crumble bread slices and soak in vinegar for 15 minutes.
2. Add all the ingredients in a blender and blend till the mixture is smooth.
3. Remove and store in a glass bottle to mature. Here, you are advised to just lick and notice the taste. It will be bitter at present.
4. Keep it in a warm place for 4-5 days and stir well.
5. Now once again lick it and see the difference in taste. As the sauce matures the taste will be sharp and sour now. This is the taste that should be achieved. The sharpness of the mustard and vinegar should give your taste buds a kind of a kick and you feel your nostrils stimulated and watery. Now your sauce is matured, so store under refrigeration.

Note: In cold weather, sauce might take a day or two longer to mature.

Usage

Mustard sauce is used with Pizzas and Burgers; mixed with other ingredients for making Sandwiches and Salad dips and dressings. Sometimes it is mixed with White sauce to bake dishes.

Preparation time: 10 minutes.

3. Cheese Cream Dressing

- Hung Curds ... *1 cup*
- Salad Oil ... *1 tsp*
  Or
- Olive Oil ... *½ tsp*
- Mustard powder... *½ -1 tsp*
- White Pepper powder ... *2 tsp*
- Sugar ... *1 tsp*
- Salt ... *1 tsp*

Preparation

1. Put all the ingredients in a bowl and mix with a spoon.
2. Chill properly before use.

Variation

Herbal Cheese Cream Dressing: Add ¼ cup chopped fresh Coriander or 1 tbsp chopped Parsley or even 2 tbsp chopped Basil to the prepared dressing.

Hung Curd is called 'Cheese Cream'.

Hung Curds: Place 3 cups home set curds in a thin cloth/ muslin cloth, tie it up and hang it for 3 hours at least. Keep a utensil underneath to collect the whey. Do not waste it as it makes an excellent soothing drink.

Healthy Drink: Chill the whey, either add Salt and Pepper to it, or 1 tbsp Rooh Afza to each glass, shake well and serve. You can also enjoy plain whey without adding anything to it, with your spicy meals.

Preparation time: 5 minutes and 30 to 40 minutes for chilling.

4. Simple French Dressing

- Table Vinegar ... *¼ cup*
- Vegetable Oil ... *¼ cup*
- Garlic Clove, crushed ... *1 no*
- Dry Mustard ... *1 tsp*
- Sugar ... *1 tsp*
- Salt & Pepper ... *to taste*

Preparation

1. Mix oil and vinegar in a glass bottle.
2. Add crushed garlic, sugar and mustard. Shake once. Add salt and pepper and shake vigorously. Chill before use.

Variation

- Instead of vinegar use Lemon juice.
- Instead of cooking oil use Olive oil.
- Make the dressing without Garlic.

Preparation time: 5 minutes only.

References

Indian Food – A Historical Companion by Dr. K.T. Achaya

The Pocket Cook Book by Elizabeth Woody

Cordon Bleu Cheese and Savouries by Macdonald and Jane's Publishers Ltd.

Vegetarian Gourmet by Dr. Paul. C. Bragg

by the same author

Nutritious Mushroom Recipes

New exotic and mouth-watering paneer dishes for all occasions.

'Foods can make or break you' is an established fact. That is why it is important to include the mushroom – one of nature's greatest wonder foods – in one's diet. Some varieties have anti-cholesterol and antibiotic properties. The common variety is full of high quality protein as well as B vitamins. With its irresistible taste, exotic flavour and rich aroma, the mushroom's delicious dishes are a healthy alternative to meat dishes. Keeping Indian tastes in mind, the author has innovated some easy-to-follow recipes.

The book contains recipes on starters, soups, salads and dishes for the main course. Some of the starters and quick stir-fried vegetable dishes of mushrooms are just ideal for tiffin boxes of children, working women and other office-goers. Most ingredients used are easily available. To retain natural taste and flavour, spices are used sparingly. Unlike some cookery books that are merely compilations, all the recipes presented here are tried, tested or innovated by the author and would be just ideal for daily meals. Besides, these dishes can easily be a part of any Indian or Continental menu set for special occasions too. In short, mushrooms used in everyday cooking will help maintain the good health of your loved ones.

Price: Rs. 96/- • Pages: 128 (Colour)
Postage: Rs. 15/-

by the same author

Paneer Bonanza

New exotic and mouth-watering paneer dishes for all occasions.

55

STARTERS • SOUPS
VEGGIES • SALADS
PIZZAS • SNACKS
DESSERTS

An invaluable treasury of traditional, yet novel recipes of Paneer distilled over 50 years of culinary knowledge and expertise.

- Easy to prepare.
- Teaches simple touches with everyday vegetables to make them special.
- Phenomenal range.

Delicious and nutritious too!

Price: Rs. 80/- • Pages: 158 + 16 Colour Pages
Postage: Rs. 15/-

by the same author

Microwave Cooking ...made easy

Innovative, yet traditional
Veg & Non-veg dishes
Indian, Continental, Chinese and Italian Cuisine

Why microwave food?

• It's faster • It's tastier
• It's nutritious • It's Convenient
• It's economical

Do you think a microwave oven's main function is to reheat leftovers? Well, think again. As a matter of fact, there is so much more you can do with it. You can easily make dishes like sarson-ka-saag, chicken tikka and momos in a jiffy, bake a cake or a pizza in minutes. Cook anything, anytime.

This small book covers:

- Useful & interesting tips
- Do's & dont's of microwave cooking
- Facts about microwave & its working
- And much more... in the simplest way possible!

Also over 100 delicious recipes for—

• Basic Pastes • Sauces • Soups • Salads • Snacks
• Breakfast • Relishes • Desserts • Main Course dishes

Enjoy healthy meals with your family and friends.

Price: Rs. 125/- • Pages: 160 (Colour)
Postage: Rs. 15/-